TREASURED
EPISTLES

Also by the Author

E.M. Forster: A Tribute
The Legacy of Nehru
Tales from Modern India
Maharaja Suraj Mal
Curtain Raisers
Profiles and Letters
The Magnificient Maharaja
Heart to Heart
My China Diary 1956–1988
Yours Sincerely
One Life Is Not Enough

TREASURED EPISTLES

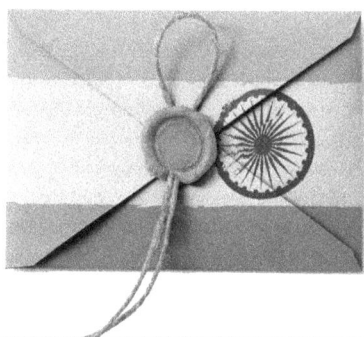

K.NATWAR SINGH

RUPA

Published by
Rupa Publications India Pvt. Ltd 2018
7/16, Ansari Road, Daryaganj
New Delhi 110002

Sales centres:
Allahabad Bengaluru Chennai
Hyderabad Jaipur Kathmandu
Kolkata Mumbai

ISBN: 978-93-5304-156-4

Second impression 2018

10 9 8 7 6 5 4 3 2

The moral right of the author has been asserted.

To
my grandsons,
Hanut and Himmat

Contents

Preface ix

I

Indira Gandhi 1–29

II

E.M. Forster 31–72

III

C. Rajagopalachari 73–93

IV

Nirad C. Chaudhuri 95–110

V

Lord Louis Mountbatten 111–126

VI

Vijaya Lakshmi Pandit 127–142

VII

Mulk Raj Anand 143–180

VIII

R.K. Narayan 181–198

IX

Krishna Hutheesing 199–218

X

Han Suyin 219–242

Preface

As a people, we are not given to preserving letters. Our indifference to history is one of the reasons for this shortcoming. I would go so far as to claim that our disregard for history is because our history of the last thousand years is, broadly speaking, not inspiring. Exceptions, however, there are. Jawaharlal Nehru is a good example. His *A Bunch of Old Letters* came out in 1960. It is still in print. Gandhiji wrote thousands of letters. Most have survived. Tolstoy's selected works run into ninety volumes. Thirty-two of them carry the letters written and received by him. Lord Curzon, as Viceroy of India, wrote a hundred-page letter to his wife in long hand. Actually, he wrote to his wife every day from Calcutta.

I had the good sense to preserve the letters published in this volume. An unknown Natwar Singh was transmuted out of the indubitably common metal that he is, to a superior product by the alchemy of the minds of indulgent and warm-hearted individuals of rare distinction and exceptional quality. For some strange reason, I got on exceptionally well with older women—Indira Gandhi, Han Suyin, Vijaya Lakshmi Pandit, Krishna Hutheesing. Not that the younger ones were neglected. Far from it. This is not, however, the place to elaborate on my love life.

I met these luminaries, whose letters are included in this volume, in my early twenties and thirties. Inevitably, each one influenced me in a different way. Consequently, my Weltanschauung[1] was vastly extended and enriched.

15 July 2018
New Delhi

K. Natwar Singh

[1] World view

I

Indira Gandhi
(1917–1984)

Ever so often, Indira Gandhi is depicted as solemn, severe, prickly and ruthless. Seldom is it mentioned that this beautiful, caring, charming, graceful and sparkling human being was a considerate humanist and a voracious reader, that she was endowed with charm, elegance, style, good taste and, above all, gravitas.

Her assassination on 31 October 1984 devastated me. The spring went out of my life. She inspired in me and Hem, my wife, a lasting affection and respect, verging on veneration. We still feel a deep sense of gratitude towards her. We owe her much. Probably, more than we can fathom.

From 1966 to 1971, I worked in her office. I saw her almost every other day, travelled the globe with her and witnessed life of the high and mighty. We gossiped, exchanged books and cracked jokes.

Let me not give the impression that she was soft or unaware of what was going on around her. She was alert, vigilant, tough—a state that could make one shiver. Her displeasure had a near paralysing effect on those who attempted to (double) cross her.

Life at the top can be lonely; presidents and prime ministers rarely have friends, leave alone political ones. But she was an exception. She did have several close (but not political) friends. One or two tried to exploit the friendship, but they paid the price.

She made two serious mistakes—declaring the Emergency in 1975 and allowing Operation Blue Star to happen. And yet, regardless of these, she was a great and powerful prime minister.

❧

28 August 1968

Dear Natwar,

As soon as I heard the good news from Secretary, I tried to speak to you on the phone, but for some reason could not get through.

Hearty congratulations to you both and blessings to the little one. May he grow up to be a source of joy and pride to you.

With every good wish.

Sincerely

(Indira Gandhi)

Motibagh Palace,
Patiala.
27 January 1970

Having failed to solve the problem of addressing you (Dear Madam, Madam, Dear Mrs Gandhi, Dear Shrimati Gandhi, Dear P.M., etc.), I have decided to send this in note form.

It is now over two weeks that I have been condemned to lie flat on my back on a hard wooden bed as a result of having slipped a disc. On the 11th, I bent down to give my son, Jagat, his teddy bear and that is when it happened. I would have thought that middle age should arrive with a little more ceremony and a little less pain. What makes it worse is being away from Delhi during these days. What makes it intolerable is that I have literally to take it lying down.

My principal pastime has been to gaze at the ceiling without having the least desire to paint it.

I should get back to work by the last week of February—Inshah Allah.

Natwar

P.M.

30 January 1970

Dear Natwar,

I knew you were on leave but I had no idea it was caused by physical incapacity to turn up. I know how painful a slipped disc can be. You have all our sympathy—however it is obviously giving you time to ruminate on the past, present and future and this is something which we all need from time to time.

You can imagine how life in Delhi is when one is facing explosive issues, and visiting VIPs during Republic Week. I am off on tour again tomorrow morning.

With every good wish for a complete recovery.

Do you remember when the same thing happened to K.P.S. Menon?[1] He had to stand in a very artistic Ajanta pose for quite some time.

Now you know the pleasures of fatherhood!

Sincerely

(Indira Gandhi)

Shri K. Natwar Singh,
Motibagh Palace, Patiala.

---

[1] Foreign Secretary, 1948–52; Ambassador to Soviet Union, 1952–61.

7 November 1970

Dear Natwar,

You certainly have done better planning than many of us. My heart has always yearned for a daughter, so I can imagine your joy in Jagat's having a baby sister.

My congratulations and good wishes to you all.

Yours sincerely,

(Indira Gandhi)

Shri K. Natwar Singh,
C-I/11 Lodi Gardens,
New Delhi.

New Delhi
26 May 1972

Dear Natwar,

Forty-one is a good age and I am glad you are facing it with equanimity. Sharda has just acquired the 'Old Age' for our library.

I have been speaking of 'The Nehru Saga' for a long time, first with Shammie Khan's husband Jamil over 15 years ago. He agreed that we could collaborate on this venture, but unfortunately he died not long after. About a month ago, I broached the subject with Bijju and Fory.[1] No takers. Anyhow, those who could have supplied really interesting tit-bits have already passed over. The great thing about the Nehru family is not the emergence of two or three famous individuals but that the large number of cousins were all distinctive in one way or another. Not only were most of them formidable characters, but the women they married also were strong personalities. It would indeed make an interesting and absorbing saga.

With good wishes to you and your family,

Sincerely

(Indira Gandhi)

Shri K. Natwar Singh,
Ambassador of India, Warsaw.

---

[1] B.K. Nehru and his wife, Fory Nehru.

22 November 1972

Dear Natwar,

Thank you for your cable and letter of birthday wishes.

I hadn't seen any books of Heinrich Böll before he got the prize. Sharada Prasad has borrowed three of his novels from a library. They have been with me on several tours but I have not got around to reading them. Another book that has followed me on my wanderings is Han Suyin's 'A Mortal Flower' lent by Bhagwan Sahay.[1] I was interested in the review of her latest book which you sent. What other type of book could she have written on Mao?

The Mao–Nixon story was new to me but the family tells me they saw it somewhere, probably in the Weekly.

I hope Hem is feeling better now.

With every good wish to you both and to Jagat and Ritu,

Yours sincerely,

(Indira Gandhi)

---

[1]Ambassador to Nepal.

24 April 1973

Dear Natwar,

I have two letters from you and the articles by the British M.P. I had noticed these myself and had thought that I should read them. In the meantime, your cuttings came and these have been travelling with me on my tours. Unfortunately, there is so much more urgent material to read that I have not got round to them yet. Perhaps, my Sri Lanka trip will give me the opportunity.

Regarding the other private letter, the Andhra issue was not helped by so many people taking interest because as you know in such matters the best of people sometimes get swayed by local pressures. Sarin[1] is doing a good job and things have improved greatly. It is too early to say whether this situation is an enduring one.

Congratulations on your 20 years of Foreign Service. They may not have been of undiluted joy but must have brought many interesting experiences.

I hope you and the family are well.

With good wishes,

Yours sincerely,

(Indira Gandhi)

Shri K. Natwar Singh,
Ambassador of India, Warsaw (Poland).

---

[1]H.C. Sarin, I.C.S.; retired as Defence Secretary and also served as Ambassador to Nepal.

12 June 1973

My dear Natwar,

I have received several letters from you. It is always when I want to send a longer reply that no reply goes.

Thank you so much for the paper-back issue of your own book and for sending the book by Paz. It is fascinating. I was just glancing through it when Borooah,[1] who is a great reader and a poet, asked me whether I had anything new to read. So I have lent the book to him.

A Delhi friend of the Joshis has sent me extracts from Joshi's letter giving details of Subhadra's[2] condition. It is most disturbing news and I am greatly worried.

Things have been extremely difficult here. Not a good time to go abroad but these visits are planned long ahead and one cannot ignore the consequences of a last minute cancellation.

Sincerely

(Indira Gandhi)

---

[1]D.K. Borooah, Congress president and Cabinet Minister. Fell out with Indira Gandhi in the late 1970s.
[2]Subhadra Joshi, freedom fighter; friend of the Nehru family.

29 May 1974

Dear Natwar,

I find two letters from you dated 7 March and 16 May in my 'To reply' file. I do not know if anybody else has acknowledged them in the meantime.

Thank you for sending me the Illich book. I have not got round to reading it or even the interview which you sent later. They are both going up to Mashobra with me on the 1st. I was greatly impressed when I met him and we got on rather well. Sharada Prasad[1] had already got the 'Tools of Conviviality' for me.

Our own blast has been successful and according to our scientists remarkably clean since the samples tested have been found to be inactive showing that there has been no radio activity. However, the blast from other countries is pretty strong as you must have seen in press reports and one does not know what fall-out there will be!

May I send you birthday greetings even though they are 13 days late. What do you mean by feeling and looking 43? It is a nice age as you will discover when you are older and you should, I hope, have more wisdom and equilibrium.

With good wishes,

Yours sincerely,

(Indira Gandhi)

---

[1] Worked with Indira Gandhi from 1964–77 and 1980–84, well-known Kannada author. Died aged 84, in 2008.

13 October 1974

Dear Natwar,

Thank you for your attempts at keeping me abreast of what people are thinking in different parts of the world. Lately, I have tended to be more engrossed in the domestic scene, which is extremely unpleasant and full of dangerous portents for our democracy and for all the ideals for which India has stood and which she has espoused in international forums.

I have been collecting interesting books, but have done little reading these last few months.

Sanjay[1] is well, although still not allowed to climb stairs and gets rather easily tired. The marriage was quiet, but dignified and elegant. Maneka[2] is a delightful girl, gay and joyous.

You have Mr Wilson[3] back with you. I wish he had more sense of humour.

Greetings,

Yours sincerely,

(Indira Gandhi)

---

[1]Sanjay Gandhi, Indira Gandhi's younger son.
[2]Wife of Sanjay Gandhi. At present, Member, Lok Sabha.
[3]Harold Wilson, Prime Minister of the UK, 1964–70, 1974–76.

4 January 1975

Dear Natwar,

Thank you for sending me Peter Jay's[1] remarks. He also wrote to me. My comment on that letter: 'a bouquet from an unexpected quarter!'

Malraux[2] was pleased with his Indian visit and I was told by the French Ambassador that he was sorry to leave.

I have glanced at Tara's[3] review of Bhatia's book. To me it seemed a rather pitiable self-portrait—so full of hatred and pettiness—of the reviewer.

P.S.: This top portion was dictated long ago but I thought I would add to it. Hence the delay. In the meantime your letter of the 27 December has come with Pam Cullen.[4] I was sorry to hear about her father. What a time to have to leave England.

Lord Louis is, as you know, incorrigible. He is friends with all the wrong sort of people and presumably believes what they tell him about me and about India. Krishna Menon[5] had something to say about this just a few days before he died.

---

[1] Well-known British journalist, editor, *The Times,* London, 1967–77. Ambassador to Washington for short while.
[2] André Malraux, author, cultural minister in General de Gaulle's cabinet. Knew Jawaharlal Nehru well.
[3] Nayantara Sahgal, daughter of Vijaya Lakshmi Pandit; she was a novelist and one of the most beautiful women of her generation.
[4] Worked in India House, London, 30 years.
[5] Krishna Menon ran India League in London from 1930 to 1947. High Commissioner to the UK, 1947–52, he was Nehru's closest foreign policy adviser, and made his reputation after his nine-hour speech on Kashmir in the UN Security Council. He was Defence Minister from 1957–62. Died in 1974, lonely and lost.

I am glad Prince Charles[6] is breaking journey here but it will be difficult to do anything interesting in just one day as I suppose the protocol part cannot be entirely ignored.

We are all stunned by L.N. Mishra's[7] murder. As the *National Herald* rightly says, although L.N.M. cannot be compared with Gandhiji in any way, there is no doubt that it was the atmosphere of hatred, calumny and violence, spread under the wings of JP[8] that was responsible for this dastardly act.

As you may have seen from the newspapers, we have had a torrent of VVIPs and international conferences—the brightest star being Gina Lolobrigida[9] who interviewed me. I believe she has also interviewed Wilson, Kissinger,[10] McNamara[11] and Fidel Castro,[12] who had urged her to meet me.

With good wishes for 1975,

Yours sincerely,

(Indira Gandhi)

---

[6]Eldest son of Queen Elizabeth II.

[7]L.N. Mishra, Commerce Minister, murdered while travelling in a train from Delhi to Patna.

[8]Jayaprakash Narayan, one of the heroes of the freedom movement. Jailed several times. Took a leading part in the Quit India Movement. At one time, considered as successor to Nehru. Later, fell out with Nehru and Indira Gandhi. Led revolt against Indira Gandhi, 1975–77. Imprisoned during Emergency.

[9]Among the most beautiful Italian and Hollywood film stars.

[10]Henry Kissinger, US President Richard Nixon's National Security Adviser and Secretary of State. Received Nobel Peace Prize for the wrong reasons.

[11]Robert McNamara, President John F. Kennedy's Secretary of State for Defence; Vietnam War hawk; President, World Bank; served on the Indira Gandhi Prize jury for five years. Died at 93, in 2009.

[12]Fidel Castro, President of Cuba from 1959 to 2006. He died in 2016.

Jammu,
14 April 1975

Dear Natwar,

Your letter of the 10th arrived only yesterday and I have just read it in the plane on the flight to Jammu.

I have not been to Jammu for a long time and since this particular visit was decided upon, new and complex problems have arisen on the political scene. Knowing the Sheikh's[1] autocratic nature, I had envisaged such a situation, though not so soon. Now we can only try to set it right and hope for the best.

In the meantime, we have given in to a part of Morarji's[2] demand—about the Gujarat elections. It seemed such a silly point for which to fast or for us to hold out, since the difference in dates was only three months. However, our difficulties are acute and varied enough without having a dead Morarji haunting the scene. One has learnt to expect all kinds of unethical action from our Opposition but I must admit that I was deeply shocked at the manner in which some of them including those in the Cong(O) seemed to view the prospect claiming that his disappearance from the scene would clear the way for Opposition unity.

It is hard going for Mother Teresa.[3] But I figured that it was

[1]Sheikh Abdullah, Chief Minister of Jammu and Kashmir several times. Spent several years in prison between 1953 and 1968.
[2]Morarji Desai, Chief Minister of Maharashtra and Central Finance Minister; Deputy Prime Minister under Indira Gandhi; and Prime Minister, 1977–79.
[3]Mother Teresa, Albania born, spent most of her life in Calcutta. An iconic missionary who received the Nobel Peace Prize for serving the poor and the destitute.

15

better for me to support a really worthwhile candidate, even if the chance of success is slim.

I am glad you have reminded me about Dame Sybil Thorndike.[4] Some time ago I had proposed that some way should be found to honour women around the world who have shown sympathy towards India. I do not know whether the Ministry has moved in the matter.

The prospect of seeing a play is indeed tempting but I do not know whether it will be possible to stop over in London.

With good wishes,

Yours sincerely,

Indira Gandhi

(Indira Gandhi)

Shri K. Natwar Singh,
Deputy High Commissioner,
India House,
Aldwych,
London W.C. 2.

---

[4]Dame Sybil Thorndike, one of the greatest British theatre personalities of the twentieth century.

Personal/Confidential
9 February 1976

Dear Natwar,

I found your letter of the 2nd awaiting me on my return from Bharatpur. We all enjoyed the trip especially as Salim Ali[1] was there and accompanied us to the sanctuary. Fortunately, I had insisted that no one else should go with us. I would have preferred to see the Dig palaces also on our own, rather than with a large gathering tagging on. A children's dance performance had also been arranged and took time which could have been used for sight-seeing.

Your brother was introduced to me very briefly, just as I was going off to the public meeting. He should have met Rajiv while I was away. But perhaps he was shy and Rajiv did not know about him.

Regarding the wall—the first step is to build along areas adjacent to villages. After that we [will] think about its extension.

I am not surprised that Subramaniam Swamy[2] is being welcomed in England. His sort would be! In India he has no influence whatsoever even in his own Party. He has not been a success in Parliament and there are often sniggers when he gets up. He seems to have a complex of some kind and is aggressive in a defensive way if you know what I mean. He is a strong advocate

---

[1]Salim Ali—perhaps India's greatest ornithologist. Nominated to the Rajya Sabha. *The Flight of a Sparrow* is his charming autobiography. Died aged 93.
[2]Maverick Indian politician.

of the Atom Bomb. He has had a long-standing quarrel with our Atomic Scientists—with Vikram Sarabhai[3] and now Sethna[4]. His main criticism was that we were quite incapable of serious work with Atomic Energy! After our experiment in Pokhran, his first reaction was that news was probably not true.

British opinion does count but if it insists on being completely cut off from the realities of the situation, there is little we can do about it except to try to educate the Indians living abroad.

Only about a hundred people were arrested in the whole of Tamil Nadu and only a few of those were political. All the important leaders are out. Even we were astonished at the good reaction all over the State.

I hope looking after the children is giving new dimension to your personality!

With good wishes,

Yours sincerely,

(Indira Gandhi)

Shri K. Natwar Singh
Deputy High Commissioner,
India House,
Aldwych, London W.C.2.

---

[3]One of India's leading atomic scientists.
[4]Homi Sethna, nuclear atomic scientist.

3 December 1976

Dear Natwar,

I always put off writing to you hoping for a more leisurely moment. But now that I am dashing off quick replies to hundreds of birthday letters, I think I shall take the opportunity of thanking you for your letter and telegram and for David Niven's[1] book. It is very relaxing.

Thank you also for passing on the book on behalf of Jennie Lee[2]. Please give her my greetings when you see her next.

Yours sincerely,

(Indira Gandhi)

Shri K. Natwar Singh,
Deputy High Commissioner,
High Commission of India,
London.

---

[1] Oscar-winning British film actor.
[2] Minister for Arts, UK, wife of A. Bevan, among eminent Labour Party leaders.

6 February 1980

Dear Natwar,

Just a line to thank you for your letter of the 17th January.

The campaign was tough and hectic but the real problems begin now. The economy is in a mess and beyond our border the dark clouds of cold war have gathered with rumblings of worst to come.

I have Kissinger's book but have not had a moment for reading for quite some time.

With good wishes,

Yours sincerely,

(signature)

(Indira Gandhi)

Shri K. Natwar Singh,
High Commissioner of India,
Lusaka.

(P.S. Thank you for the *Time* cutting and cartoon. I had seen it but am glad to have another copy.)

9 June 1980

Dear Natwar,

Your letter of the 4th.

Just when you are talking about the working of the democratic process in a coherent way, Badshah Khan[1] is busy giving statements from a Srinagar Hospital that there is no democracy in India and compares us in a vague sort of way to Pakistan! Can you believe it? All this keeps one from getting a swollen head.

We have won the elections but the going was pretty tough and many of the seats either won or lost, were neck-to-neck.

The real difficulties now begin. The people's expectations are high but the situation both political or economic, is an extremely complex one. I cannot help being an optimist and I have no doubt that if only our legislators and the people as a whole have the patience and forbearance to climb the steep and stony path for the next few months, we can get over the hump and arrive at a place from which progress is possible once again.

However, politics is at a low ebb. All those who shouted so much about democracy have no compunctions now in saying as Charan Singh[2] has, that 'Parliament is irrelevant', or the Jan Sangh encouraging anti-national elements in the North-East. The Opposition parties are making frantic efforts, egged on by

---

[1]Khan Abdul Ghaffar Khan, also known as Frontier Gandhi. Served many years in jail before 1947 and thereafter in Pakistani jails. Died aged 98.
[2]Charan Singh, Chief Minister, Uttar Pradesh; Deputy Prime Minister and Prime Minister between 1977–80. Died 1987.

21

Bahuguna[3], to unite. What for? Only to have agitations and violence or to encourage defections.

I am glad you are enjoying Islamabad.

Yours sincerely,

(Indira Gandhi)

Shri Natwar Singh,
High Commissioner of India,
Islamabad.

---

[3]H.N. Bahuguna, MP and former Chief Minister of UP.

3 August 1981

Dear Natwar,

I have read some of the interviews in the book you left and I am depressed. I feel isolated, not because of policies, the correctness of which will be seen in time as it has been before. But while the earth spins on the beauty and with method, the world of men is a hollow one, where words have no meaning and sentiments no feeling, the young have lost wonder, elan and even hope. What can a leaden-eyed civilisation do? Can a flame of idealism or a vision of a better man be protected from all this cynicism, hypocrisy and hatred?

8 August 1981

I did not send this as I thought you were coming to Delhi. I am sorry to hear you are unwell and in hospital. Do get well soon.

Thank you for Galbraith's[1] book though I have it already. We might exchange—you can take mine as it has no name on it.

Sincerely

(Indira Gandhi)

---

[1] John Kenneth Galbraith, economist, bestselling author; served as US Ambassador to India during presidency of John F. Kennedy. Died aged 97.

25 August 1981

Dear Natwar,

Just when you were due to return from London we heard that you were unwell and in hospital. I thought you would stop by in Delhi on your way to Islamabad. But it seems you have gone direct.

How was your meeting in London? The question of the Secretary-General seems to be in a flux again. The Soviets do not like Salim[1] because they think he is pro-China. Waldheim[2] has been throwing his weight around in Nairobi and elsewhere and was telling everyone that the OAU decision was taken in the early hours of the morning when many Heads of States were not present, so that there is likelihood of division in their ranks. I do not know if this development improves Ramphal's[3] chances, for I am told that Latin Americans do not regard him as representative of their area.

---

[1] Salim Ahmed Salim, Tanzanian politician. Educated in India, he became Foreign Minister and then Prime Minister of Tanzania.
[2] Kurt Waldheim; UN Secretary General. Later, President of Austria.
[3] Shridath Surendranath Ramphal; Secretary General of the Commonwealth.

I have your books with me—the Galbraith one and the one that you lent me.

I hope you are quite well now.

Sincerely

(Indira Gandhi)

Shri K. Natwar Singh
Ambassador of India
Islamabad.

18 November 1982

Dear Natwar,

Thank you for your birthday greetings. But I am disappointed that there was no good story to enliven my day. Have you read Norman Cousin's[1] book on his illness, giving positive proof that laughter is the best and sometimes the only medicine?

Sincerely

(signature)

(Indira Gandhi)

Shri Natwar Singh
Secretary
Ministry of External Affairs
New Delhi.

---

[1]Well-known editor of *Saturday Review*, New York.

18 March 1983

Dear Natwar,

I write to express my appreciation of your work for the Non-Aligned Meeting. Now that it is over we can safely say that our fears and apprehensions regarding the shortness of time and a myriad other difficulties were unfounded, or perhaps provided the motivation to redouble our efforts. That the meeting was an unqualified success is confirmed by all. Please also convey my appreciation to all members of your team.

You shouldered a heavy responsibility and bore it cheerfully. But this is the beginning, and the next three years will be full of problems and difficulties. We must maintain the team spirit and start planning for the successful fulfilment of the 'Delhi Declaration'.

With good wishes,

Yours sincerely,

(Indira Gandhi)

Shri Natwar Singh
Secretary,
Ministry of External Affairs,
New Delhi.

14 December 1983

Dear Natwar,

I have been meaning to write ever since the Commonwealth Heads of Governments left but each day has been busier than the last.

CHOGM[1] was another successful demonstration of our organisational capability and of the team spirit which we are able to muster on special occasions. As Chief Coordinator, you shouldered the bulk of the responsibility. I want to congratulate you on the smooth functioning of the meetings at all levels and for the excellent arrangements. Please convey my congratulations to all the members of your team.

With good wishes,

Yours sincerely,

(Indira Gandhi)

Shri Natwar Singh,
Secretary (PC),
Ministry of External Affairs,
New Delhi.

---

[1]Commonwealth Heads of Government Meeting

8 August 1984

Dear Natwar

I am so sorry to hear of your illness. I hope it is not too painful but I am told one has to be very careful for a long time.

Get well soon,

Yours sincerely,

(Indira Gandhi)

Shri K. Natwar Singh

II

E.M. Forster
(1879–1970)

As I write, affectionate recollections of E.M. Forster come rushing to my mind. I do not wish to drive them away. It is to him that I owe whatever awakening has befallen me. I have said elsewhere that a part of myself, such as it is, has been influenced by him. I do not know if that would do him any credit.

My college—Corpus Christi College, Cambridge—was less than a five-minute walk to King's College where Forster lived. In the last two decades of his life, he attained 'Gurudom'. His admirers from all parts of the world dropped in to pay homage. As the months passed, our friendship deepened. Published in 1924, I had read A Passage to India *and had questioned him about it. 'What were the reactions in Britain on its publication?' I had asked him. Forster had replied, 'For a long time no one took notice. Then,* The Morning Post *reviewed it favourably... then followed critical and wholly welcome praise.' The book is still in print. It has sold nearly a million and a half copies and has been translated in almost all European languages.*

A Passage to India *is not my favourite Forster novel. It would be* Howards End *(1910).*

Forster's essay, 'What I Believe', is one of the most stirring pieces of writing in the English language. I agree with 90 per cent of what he wrote, but not with the following: 'I hate the idea of causes, and if I had to choose between betraying my country and betraying my friend, I hope I should have the guts to betray my country... Love and loyalty to an individual can run counter to the claims of the State. When they do—down with the State, say I, which means that the State would down me.'

I got to know Forster very well at Cambridge in the early 1950s. On his 85th birthday in 1964, I edited a book of tributes. The contributors were Mulk Raj Anand, Ahmed Ali, Raja Rao, Narayan Menon, Santha Rama Rau and myself. The volume was published by Forster's American publishers, Harcourt, Brace and Jovanovich. It was a success without being a financial disaster.

King's College
Cambridge

5 February 1954

Dear Mr Natwar Singh,

Thank you for the enclosures which I have read with much interest.

I shall be most happy to come to the Majlis dinner on the 22nd. The only thing is that I am booked that day to speak to the India Society. I hope and expect that the India Society will be cancelling its meeting, so that its members can attend the dinner. Perhaps, you could kindly have a word with its Secretary, and ask him to let me know.

It was very nice meeting you the other day and I hope we may soon meet again.

Yours ever,

(E.M. Forster)

16 March 1954

Dear Mr Natwar Singh,

Thank you for sending me Mr Thakur's[1] plays. They are both fanciful and thoughtful. I should think the first one might be effective on the stage. The second one is rather static and it challenges certain comparisons with *Animal Farm* which it cannot sustain, but it should be quite an entertaining drama for school boy actors and audiences. I don't find either play very satisfactory philosophically, but this may be because what little philosophy, I have in me is westernised.

I can't get a copy of *Hindoo Holiday* either. I cannot even find my own! I am ordering one, and when it arrives I shall be very pleased to lend it to you.

With all good wishes, and with thanks,

Yours sincerely,

(E.M. Forster)

---

[1]N.G. Thakur, Housemaster and Vice-Principal, Scindia School, Gwalior. A great teacher.

15 April 1954

Dear Mr Natwar Singh,

I was so pleased to get your letter and thank you for what you say about 'The Hill of Devi' and your correction on points of detail. The spelling of Scindia in this country seems very wild. Yes I am afraid the book will be as uncongenial to the new India as 'A Passage ....' was to the old 'Anglo-India'. The outlook of both books is much the same, I think. It is the political situation that has altered. I am sorry, though, to have given the impression of denigrating Gandhiji. I wish Congressmen could have heard the short speech I made about him in the Union here, after his murder, they might have been better pleased.

I have bought a copy of 'Hindoo Holiday', partly to have the pleasure of lending it to you—when can you come around for it? I shall be in on Saturday at about 6.30 p.m. if that happens to suit you.

Yours sincerely,

(E.M. Forster)

King's College
Cambridge

17 May 1954

Dear Natwar,

Thank you so much for the book, it looks most interesting. When can you come and write in it? Can you come and have some lunch next Friday (the 21) at 1.00 p.m.?

Yours very sincerely,

(E.M. Forster)

Cambridge

20 June 1954

Dear Natwar,

Dinner on Friday the 23rd would be delightful and I will come along at 7.30 p.m. to 8.00 p.m. unless I hear to the contrary. So, get going with your Batterie de Cuisine. I do not know when I come up but will easily find my way to you. Thank you very much. It will be very nice seeing you again.

With love,

Yours,

(E.M. Forster)

King's College
Cambridge

18 July 1954

My dear Natwar,

I do trust I am writing to the correct address. Some confusion in my papers. I will put my address on the envelope, too, so that this may be returned to me if necessary, and I may start again.

I am coming up on Friday the 23rd which doesn't leave much time to start again, and am more or less free most of Saturday. I would love to come to a meal with you, if convenient, and I know I shall enjoy your cooking.

As for a play, I too have seen 'I am a Camera' and Dorothy Tutin[1] is indeed good. But Van Druten[2] has turned Isherwood's[3] wonderful hand-made stories into the machine made and the mass produced. All the distinctive atmosphere of rising Nazism has gone (however I have just been here to a far more mechanical play—'The Burning Glass').

I hear the Cambridge boy's review *Out of the Blue* or some such name is very funny, but why need we go to play. Let's just eat and eat. (Alternately). Friday evening might be a possibility—In haste and with love.

Yours,
Morgan Forster

---

[1]British film actress.
[2]Theatre director.
[3]Christopher Isherwood, author of *Goodbye to Berlin* and book on Vedanta. Among close younger friends of Forster.

Cambridge

21 August 1954

Dear Natwar,

This is news indeed, and indeed sad news.[1] I am here all this week and more or less free until Friday. Could you come up to lunch on Wednesday? Failing that, what do you suggest?

I returned here yesterday, motored in two days and a bit from Bayreuth to Boulogne and feel a little dazed but very well.

With love and hoping to hear your plans soon,

Morgan

---

[1] The sad news Forster refers to here is of my transfer to India.

Dear Natwar,

I have become a shocking correspondent in these days, but here is a line to say I shall be happy for you to reprint my tribute to Nehru in the '*Illustrated Weekly*'—I haven't kept a copy.

I don't envy you your elections, ours are just over, and not so awfully. The only thing in them that really upset me was the Smethwick result.

With love and I am so glad you now have your parents happy.

Morgan

My dear Natwar,

Thank you for your p.c., your letter, and the photograph of us. The last has only just arrived for Stearns have been most dilatory and muddling. I called for it today and told them to forward the two other copies to you, by surface mail. The next thing is a ring for me (in my absence) saying that they have lost your address. I am giving it tomorrow and the copies shall reach you—in? Ten days? Thereabout anyhow. Let me know if they don't come.

I hope you will approve of my choice between the proofs, but there really was no choice. The full face one was awful—we looked like a couple of frying pans. The profiles (which you will receive) at any rate suggest human beings. I am looking at you and you are looking away from me. Rather unreciprocal and I wish we had been able to get taken at the K.P. Shop. Stearns is too much on mass-production lines.

I was interested on your experiences on the boat. The world is pretty frightening, isn't it? One comes out of one's own little corner expecting the world to bear some resemblance to it, and lo! Tea Planters and their wives.

I have noticed the books you mention. Ian Stephens[1] had just lent me a novel by a man called Masters[2]. It is not attractive but deals with a subject that interests me. Mixture of races.

Please write again and tell me how Hem and you are getting down. I am very well myself.

With love,

Yours affectionately,
E.M. Forster

---

[1] Long-time editor, *The Statesman*. Became fellow of King's College, Cambridge.
[2] John Masters, ex-Indian Army and author of *Bhawani Junction*.

Dear Natwar,

It was nice to hear from you, but really the photographs are incredible. I have been at them twice, on one occasion repeating your address which they had lost and I don't think I can do any more, they only gape.

I suggest your writing severely to them, registering your letter, and quoting the number which is penciled on my own copy: S3645A. If you still cannot get a reply from them then I suppose I shall have to give you my copy, but I shall not do so with any pleasure as I like it. Their address: Stearn and Sons Photographers, Sidney Street, Cambridge.

Thank you for the Christmas Card. I am not sending any this year, only bits of paper like this: but it brings my love and best wishes for your happiness. You sound to be having an excellent time. How I wish I was a cultural Chinese to go with you on that tour.

I have not much news. I have just been to a feast at New College Oxford, and was deeply impressed by the gravity and dignity of the College and of its architecture. King's looked a bit too ostentatious when I returned. 'Look at me, Royal'. New College did not mind whether one looked or not.

I have finished or almost finished *Bhawani Junction*: I shall never finish it quite as the Colonel's copulations became too much or rather too many for me... The railway, the people, rail loyalty, Anglo-Indianism—all that was excellent and India should welcome it, though might find it difficult to do so. My chief sub-continental pleasure has however been Stella Kramrisch's[1] book on Indian Art.

Well, goodbye for the present, Natwar, and please write again. I have seen a little of Hutheesing[2] this term. What a nice chap he is!

With love and hoping to see you again before too long,

Morgan

---

[1]Curator of Indian art at the Philadelphia Museum of Art and Professor of Indian art at the Institute of Fine Arts, New York University, for many years. Wrote *The Presence of Shiva* and *The Art of India*.
[2]Harsh Hutheesing, elder son of Krishna Hutheesing—the youngest sister of Jawaharlal Nehru.

Cambridge

1 April 1955

My dear Natwar,

I am a shocker over writing. Even now I haven't told you how much I liked the thing about me, and even now I don't return it for it has got hidden under something or other in this all too capacious apartment. I trust you have a copy. In any case I will hunt for it again. It is here and it did give me great pleasure.

Now I get your line about Mr Chaudhuri[1]. I had a letter from the British Council earlier in the day. They suggested our meeting, and I replied to them that if he cared to write to me direct I should hope to fix something. It's up to him to write, I think, after the way he snubbed my poor Aziz[3]. They tell me he has been invited over here by the B.B.C. to collect material for broadcasts.

Everything here is right except the weather. East wind all day and frost most nights. I keep well and am beginning to see the end of my work. Until its back is broken I don't feel inclined to go abroad, though the French opportunities have offered themselves. An old friend of mine, Ahmed Ali[3] has been over from Karachi, and since last I saw him he has become an expert on China. One

---

[1]Nirad C. Chaudhuri, author of *The Autobiography of an Unknown Indian*. Died in 1999, aged 101.
[2]A leading character in E.M. Forster's *A Passage to India*, whom Nirad Chaudhuri had severely criticized in an article on Forster in *Encounter* magazine in 1954.
[3]Author of *Twilight in Delhi*. Migrated to Pakistan in 1947.

result of this is that he has given me a Sung saucer.

Well, I must finish this chatter and go to bed. I recently spent a very pleasant evening with Hutheesing. Have also met Mrs Pandit[4] and was quite bowled over, of course. And finally, I have just been to the Boat Race.

With love,

Yours

(E.M. Forster)

[4]Vijaya Lakshmi Pandit, sister of Nehru. President, UN General Assembly, 1953–54. Also, Ambassador to the Soviet Union and USA. Died in 1990.

30 June 1955

My dear Natwar,

Your merited reprimand caused further frantic search here, and here is your article.... But it is dangerous to send people of my age anything which it is hoped to see back again.

I liked Mr Chaudhuri—thought him so first hand and it was remarkable how much and how genuinely he was enjoying English eighteenth century homes, the pictures of Domenico Veneziano. Now there is another excitement—a novelist called Mr Pendse, who had never travelled farther than Bombay and is here under the Rockefeller Foundation. What do you think of him? For, I expect you know all about him. Ian Stephen and I liked him very much, and I find his novel—translated and badly translated as 'The Sky is the Limit'—very moving and entirely free of 'isms'. I wish I could help it to a publisher in this country. There was also to be a third Indian—name forgotten and somehow very much the Good Boy—who failed to reach Cambridge because of the strike—and my old friend Ahmed Ali has been over from Karachi.

That concludes my sub-continental news. Coming nearer home. I have had an attack of gout—a distinguished ailment but I wish it had not selected the Aldebourgh Festival. I did not let it hold me back, but attended concerts, opera, mystery plays and cocktail parties with one foot in a khaki-coloured slipper, and was dragged down to the sea on my back on a mackintoshed rug, leaving a deep furrow in the shingle. It is better now. I hope to remain at Cambridge for the next six weeks, and then have a fortnight's motoring in France.

I do hope that your eyes are giving no more trouble and that life is now alright with you generally.

With love,

Yours,

(E.M.F.)

I am trying to finish off my great..........book, and hope I may do so by the autumn. Until it is off my chest I would rather not read any more MS—so please excuse me to your late teacher. E.M.F.

Dear Natwar,

Just an unornamented Christmas and New Year Card to wish you all happiness in both. I am spending both events in Coventry—then via Cambridge to Aldebourgh. I was glad to get your letter, with its fascinating glimpse of your visitors. I do not wonder that the Russians have won the stakes. They give India help of the type that was refused by Europe, and they profit by Europe's suicidal racial arrogance. In time they too will develop racialism but—though there are already sings of it—the time is not yet.

The review of Malhotra[1] pleased me rather than not. Why did you think so badly of it? As I have fared much worse in the past, both orientally and accidentally—I never like to refuse interviews connected with India; my heart in this direction is too tender. Last week it was a Mr Jyoti with a numerous schedule of questions about mysticism. Let us see what Mr Jyoti produces.

With all the best for 1956,

Morgan

---

[1]Inder Malhotra, well-known journalist and author of the biography of Indira Gandhi.

Dear Natwar,

Do you remember my once saying that I gave a short address at a meeting in the Union, after Mahatma Gandhi's murder? Some copies of the text have just turned up. I should like to send you one, if I may. It is a little expression of what I felt at the time, and indeed still feel.

I have mislaid your last letter. I was so very sorry to hear of your sad family news[1] in it, and I had intended to write before.

I have kept well, my book is out (biography of an aunt: the sort of subject the English are willing to spend much time over), and I have been to Greece. We spent a charming day on Santori, and are distressed by the tragic news. It did look a fantastic and insecure place. The water was too deep for anchorage, and the boat had to lie on the walls of crater and keep the engines going to toughen the ropes. The Greeks were all charming, particularly our own Greek friends. It was not like the newspapers at all. What indeed is?

Friends of Natwar's look in from time to time. Some of them, I suspect, know him better than do others. There has been a very pleasant intelligent Singh at Trinity—I forget his initials: training for the foreign service, I think he talked most interestingly about Indian painting, and has told me the subject of a little miniature which I possess and which I have never interpreted.

The International P.E.N. Conference is in progress in London. I have behaved rather shamefully, but go up to it tomorrow and on Saturday entertain about 20 members to tea here. (Sardar

---

[1] He was referring to my father's heart attack.

Panikkar[2] should have been member of Honour for India, but according to the latest rumour he has popped off to Poland, leaving, disgruntlement behind him.)

Well, I will conclude now, with love, and with hope of my soon seeing you again.

Morgan

P.S.: I saw much of Harsha towards the end of his time here; much to my pleasure.

---

[2]K.M. Panikkar, courtier, author, diplomat. As Ambassador to China, flouted government instructions—changed sovereignty to suzerainty relating to Tibet.

C.C.

19 October 1956

My dear Natwar,

What a lovely gift and how kind of Dr Bredsdorff to convey it. He could not stay long, but gave me little news of you, and I gathered from it and from your letter that Pekin[1] is not too bad, and any how interesting. 'A hundred schools of thought' is a cheering edict. Unfortunately there is always the 101st.

There are two schools of thought only about your scroll. Dr Bredsdorff maintained it should be hung horizontally. I surely am right in upholding it perpendicular and I shall do so pending your ruling to the contrary. We sought a third opinion from the birds, as to which way they would prefer their heads to hang, but they didn't seem to mind.

I have just been to the Russian Ballet, and found it well upto its fame. I have also—a quieter experience—passed a week in Holland amidst dykes and lakes and I saw the remarkable Rembrandt Exhibition.

Well, I must end now and I hope and I hope readably, for I lost my pen on the boat and lack the energy to buy a new one.

With love and thanking you most warmly for the delightful present.

Yours ever,
Morgan Forster

---

[1]Peking—not yet Beijing.

3 December 1956

My dear Natwar,

Your bounties crowd upon me. On the heels of two charming little birds, swaying gracefully on their branch arrive four magnificent dragons. Mr Nehru was most kind to deliver them, and I have seen him since, and I have also seen Mr Gokhale.[1] Each of them was able to give me a little news of you, and I hope that you are keeping fairly well and cheerful, considering the sad family loss that you have undergone.

I keep all right myself—considering my age and the state of world.

With love and all kind greetings for Christmas and the New Year and with my thanks,

Yours ever,

(E.M. Forster)

---

[1]Ashok Balachandra Gokhale. Joined Indian Foreign Service (IFS), 1955.

20 December 1956

My dear Natwar,

Affectionate Christmas greetings and did I thank you for the sumptuous embroidered dragons? I can't be sure, I know I thanked you for the delicate little birds on whose heels they had followed. It is most kind and generous of you.

Like most people, I am pretty gloomy in the days. So will stop. Gloomers are bores. I am off to the midlands for Christmas, back in the New Year to go to Britten's[1] new opera at Covent Garden.

With love and again thanks for your generous and acceptable gifts.

Yours ever,

(E.M. Forster)

---

[1]Benjamin Britten, famous British conductor, composer and pianist.

Dear Natwar,

How sweet of you to remember my birthday! I send you a line of greeting on it for 1957. We all need each other's greetings for the world is in a strange state, and the things I have always thought valuable are not only ignored in China but deprecated in this country. I expect that a few islets in Cambridge and elsewhere will remain uncovered for longer than I shall, so I don't worry personally which is in all circumstances a mistake. Still, when I reflect what the human race might do and feel, and observe what people do and how they don't feel, I naturally get depressed.

I am sorry to hear of your throat and hope it has cleared up permanently. I am all right myself. I am in Coventry for the moment and go tomorrow to London (shortly to be renamed Londong) to see Britten's new ballet. Then to Cambridge. Yes, Ravi Shankar was marvellous, so was the tabla boy. They came to Cambridge, too, but all went there most vexatious. I was laid up and couldn't go, and the wretched secretary did absolutely nothing until the last minute. I had actually to write to London to find out where tickets could be got. Consequently, the big room in the Union was almost empty, and the people who could have filled it either didn't know or were engaged and have in either case since been tearing their hair. Nothing enrages me like an insult to a great artist coupled with a deprivation to the public, and for that reason I shall end this letter by giving the secretary's name: M.V. Das of Queens.

It will, indeed, be nice if you got over to this country before long. Meanwhile, every good wish and love.

(E.M. Forster)

My dear Natwar,

I was greatly touched by your letters, and by their proof of your affection for me. Yes—I am a good age by this time, and life is uncertain for me, as of course, it is for every one. But it is a great consolation to know, while one is still alive, that one is liked and valued, and the mistake about my death has procured me this. The novelist, Joyce Carey, died the day you heard the rumour and I thought there might have some confusion between us: but you say the man's name was actually Forster; there was a classical scholar of the name, I know.

Your accounts of the spoil-sport state fascinate me. When I try to conjecture the immediate future of this energetic planet, I am divided between interest and gloom. All the values I appreciated are disappearing and I don't want to outlive them: at the same time it has been fascinating to watch the growth of man's physical powers during the past half century—after millards of preparation during which so little changed.

Oh dear, I did not mean to write a letter like this, or quite like it. I am going to Austria next month for a fortnight. This is my proximate festivity, with two friends. I fly to Zurich: then train to Innsbruck, Salzburg and Linz: thence down the Danube to Vienna whence we fly back to London.

I like your unshaven photograph so much and it is on the mantel shelf. Thanks also for the one with Mrs. Hutheesing.

I miss Harsha. Also you! The Indian I see most of is a Maratha, who is apprenticed at Pye's, and knows a great deal about music. P.S.: I am writing in London actually. I have been to the R.A. banquet, and am still sleepy from it. Much love and I should think you now might achieve calling me Morgan.

Morgan

My dear Natwar,

It is indeed high time I wrote to you. I shall have you not writing any more, if I don't. I had satisfactory news from Mrs Hutheesing about you yesterday. She seemed well on the spot. Was just on her way with her other son to collect Harsha out of Princeton.

Thank you for your Chinese letters and for the two China books. I have not made much way of them yet. I do not know much about things Chinese—but the lovely embroidery you previously gave me is still with me. I use it as a bed-spread, for which it is far too good, but one gets a little reckless with property as one grows old, it will in any case last one out.

My health is very good at present: Greece and Turkey had an excellent effect on it, and except for some deafness I really have nothing to complain off. We are in the full swing of the May week activities—balls, concerts, parties, informal drinks of young people sitting in masses on the grass. I attend a suitable proportion of these. The best item is however over—the recital last Thursday by Vilayat Khan in the Union. I thought him marvellous. He went on, with one small break, for 3/4 hours and had us all entranced. For the first section he used the Yamani Raga. How I wish I understood the damn stuff better. I never shall. I am surely convinced that it is great. He performs again at the Aldeburgh Festival. So do I, unfortunately not at the same date.

I haven't much plans for the future—a vague one to go to Venice, but all European outings depend on what happens in France. Hitherto de Gaulle has done what the army tells him, however the propagandists wrap it up. Let us see what happens if he does something the army doesn't want him to do. Let us see what happens if he dies.

However, here I am writing about politics to you who are in them and presumably sick of them. Please write to me about them or anything else.

With love,
Morgan

My dear Natwar,

A line—which ought to have come before, but advancing years make one slack—to thank you for your good and seasonable wishes, also for your nice article on me; though am I all that shy? My birthday festivities went well, and I enjoyed them, and they ended in quite a magnificent concert given by the College Musical Society. I keep very good health for my age, and I hope you do for yours.

I have just finished B. Rajan's[1] 'The Dark Dancer'. What do you think of it? I am much impressed. I have seen a proof copy of Chaudhuri's 'Passage to England'. What a talented but spikey chap he is? He actually goes out of his way to warn us British against the myth of Indo-British friendship, which I do think is a bit much. I must try to find out something more about him, apart from what he himself tells.

Harsha is out of college and working hard I fancy—any how I don't see as much of him as I should like. Mrs Pandit has passed with benignity. There has been some good Indian music. And I have tried to talk to the Cambridge Majlis, but the exigencies of influensa have compelled us to postpone till next term.

Oh! yes, and Mahalenobis[2] of Calcutta has become Hon. Fellow of King's College—that's all the strictly or semi-strictly Indian news that I can think of, so I will now conclude with my love.

Yours ever,
E.M. Forster

---

[1] Balchandra Rajan. Joined IFS, 1948. Resigned, 1961.
[2] P.C. Mahalenobis—physicist, statistician and member, Planning Commission.

My dear Natwar,

Many thanks for your flattering but affectionate article in 'The Times of India'. I like it so much. I have also had some welcome letters from you lately, and have been intending to write to you, but all the news there is about me, you seem already to know. I still sit about quietly, still have no telephone and though I have gramophone, it does not revolve as quickly as it should: probably needs cleaning. My chief expedition last year was to Germany—driving from Holland to Austria via devious and unfrequented roads, very leafy and soothing. Some of the architecture—e.g. Vierzehnheiligen[1] is earth shaking. I was quite unprepared for it. This year—all being well I go to Italy in June and France in September. So, let us hope that all continues well and that there is a France and Italy to go to.

Do let me know when you are over here, as I suppose you may be, and have the time to meet me in Cambridge or London. It will be so nice to be talking together again. I see Harsha when he is around— always a pleasure but I never know when it will be.

Well, I will end now, with affectionate wishes and love from Morgan. (The story of the comparison between Charles Morgan[2] and myself is not apocryphal. I am the sole, the reliable authority for it. But it has been apocryphallically extended.)

I forgot to mention the Queen—the poor things are always on the move in these days: but she should find India something special.

Morgan

---

[1]This pilgrimage church was built by Balthasar Neumann, one of the greatest architects of the eighteenth century.
[2]British novelist.

9 August 1961

My dear Natwar,

I am so pleased to hear from you, and to know that you have got through your operation. I have had troubles, too, and I too have got through them. This is just to say that I shall be in Cambridge on exactly 20 August and I hope that there will be an opportunity of seeing you, if only for a moment. A few days later I am off to France.

With best love and what a nice letter.

Morgan

21 November 1961

My dear Natwar,

Thank you for your nice letters and photographs of myself. The one you took of mine in a red tie is superb. The one of me with an oriental animal was taken by Mohsin Ali, now in Reuters, and strangely enough I heard from him recently.

Santha Ram Rau[1] seems doing marvels over Passage to Broadway and I have also had an encouraging talk with its producer over here. You urge me to come over for the opening performance and also to take care of myself. I wish one could combine these incompatibles.

With affectionate remembrances,

Morgan

PS: It is unfortunate about your friend J. Ivory. All was fixed for his visit but I went down with influensa and I had to write and put them off—he was bringing friends.

---

[1] Spent most of her life in the USA. Best known Indian novelist in America from 1950 to 1960. Wrote the script of the theatre version of *A Passage to India*. It was a considerable success in London and New York.

My dear Natwar,

What an agreeable idea, and may I be here in 1964 the more fully to appreciate it. It would be excellent to include with a covering word, my words about Gandhiji for I don't think they are widely known.

My Hyderabad friends would be interested, particularly those connected with the 'Urdu House' there—I sent a donation to it from my takings of 'The Passage' performance in New York. And speaking of Hyderabad a book on me has been written by a Dr V.A. Shahane[1] who is professor of English in the Osmania University there. I am delighted with it—one of the best studies on me, I thought, and very well informed. Do have a look at it if it comes your way—published by Kitab Mahal, Lahore, if my memory serves. I haven't a copy to hand.

I keep fairly well thanks and look forward to a play on 'Where Angels Fear to Tread', which goes on here at the end of the month. Dramatised by Mrs Elizabeth Hart (American). I think she has done it very well. Bryan Shaw produces it.

I hope that you too keep well.

With love,

Yours ever,

(E.M. Forster)

P.S.: My kindest remembrances to Santha Ram Rau when you see her.

---

[1]Forster scholar from Hyderabad; author of *E.M. Forster: A Reassessment*.

17 June 1963

Dear Natwar,

I received your kind letter on my return from France—a particularly agreeable France.

I don't think I ought to edit a tribute to myself—or indeed to contribute to it except by my long-ago tribute to Gandhiji which I am very glad should appear.

So I am not reading what Mulk[1] writes about me.

I have not heard from H.B.[2] of this pleasant project and do not see why I should. I am not interested, (here) in that side of the thing. It has my affectionate approval and I shall be glad if it contains an element of surprise. Tell them not to send me any contracts. I require no payment for the Gandhi speech or for anything else. I should feel it unseemly.

Yours ever,
Morgan

P.S.: We have now had our telephone talk. It will be better not to attempt it again as I have no phone in my room, and much running about on the part of porters is involved.

---

[1]Mulk Raj Anand, prolific novelist. Forster helped with the publication of his first novel, *Untouchable*.
[2]Harcourt Brace—publishers of the Forster tribute volume.

16 July 1963

Dear Natwar,

I could scarcely refuse to read your Tribute when you asked me to do so, and I have read it with much pleasure. I expect to do the same with the others when the time comes and I shall then write separately to all who have paid me this honour.

To turn to the less pleasant subject of your Harcourt contract, I hope that my 'concession' has arrived and been helpful. I must now ask you not to refer any further business troubles to me. I cannot assist you over them for the reason that I have already given all the help that is in my power.

With every good wish,

Yours ever,
Morgan

King's College
Cambridge

24 July 1963

My dear Natwar,

I asked you in my last letter to stop the publishers from writing to me, but expect I did not give you the time to for here comes a letter from Iovanowich.[1] I enclose a copy of my reply. It looks to me as if Miss Rau's agent has been trying to be clever-clever.

When the pleasant project of a birthday tribute was started I assumed that it was a personal courtesy from Indians to an Englishman and did not realise that American publicity methods would be called in. To the tribute itself I continue to look forward.

With good wishes to all the contributors,

Yours ever,
Morgan

---

[1]Owner of Harcourt Brace publishing house.

Cambridge

10 August 1963

Dear Natwar,

I am afraid that the title you mentioned (Only Connect) does not seem to me appropriate to this type of book and I have informed Harcourt Brace accordingly. The book is an offering from writers to a writer and I wish to come out clearly in its title. 'Tribute to E.M. Forster' is the sort of thing.

With all good wishes and much appreciation of the trouble you have taken.

Yours ever,
Morgan

Cambridge

21 August 1963

My dear Natwar,

Thank you for your letter of the 14th. I was sorry not to accept 'Only Connect', which as a title is effective but unsuited to this particular book. Your alternative of 'E.M. Forster – a Tribute from India' is exactly right, but for the omission of Pakistan, Ahmed Ali, as you say, must be considered—indeed it is generous of him to come in. Do you think it might be possible to put on the title page (not of course on the exterior of the book) something like:

E.M. Forster—A Tribute from friends in India and in Pakistan?

If you do, perhaps you would discuss it with the publishers.

I am so glad you like Shahane's book. I haven't read that particular James Baldwin[1] yet. Fascinating colour-news about the U.N.

With love and thanks for all the trouble you have taken,

Morgan

---

[1] American novelist.

14 November 1963

My dear Natwar,

Thank you so much for your note and for the enclosure relating to your own other good work.

I can't tell you how much I am looking forward to the book. With love,

Morgan

Dear Natwar,

The advance copy has just arrived and couldn't have done so at a time more convenient to me. For I am just off for a fortnight, and read the other contributions and can write to the other contributions while I am away. I am much pleased with the appearance of the book, and with the editing. The selection from my own writing looks excellent and must have meant a great deal of work. Many of my own remarks about India I had quite forgotten.

I must stop now and consider packing and a journey through cold weather.

With love and renewed thanks,

Yours ever,
Morgan

P.S.: I liked your contribution as I said.

My dear Natwar,

I have now written to all the others* and before midnight strikes there shall be this renewed line of gratitude to you. What a splendid piece of work—the contributions so welcome and the 'anthology' so sensitively and intelligently chosen and marshalled with such skill. The publishers, too come out so well.

A happy New Year to you shall attend my thanks. And I note with pleasure that Mr Faubion Bowers[1], whom I met over here, has accorded assistance. Please convey my appreciation to him.

With love and most sincere thanks,

Morgan

*Mulk Raj Anand, Ahmed Ali, Narayana Menon[2], Raja Rao[3] and Santha Ramu Rau.

---

[1]Husband of Santha Rama Rau, was Aide-de-Camp (ADC) to General MacArthur after Japan's defeat in 1945.

[2]Narayan Menon got to know Forster during World War II, while working with the BBC in London. Wrote a book on W.B. Yeats, which Forster reviewed for the BBC.

[3]Author of *Kanthapura* and *The Serpent and the Rope*. Knew Forster well.

1 April 1964

My dear Natwar,

Thank you very much for the 'Old Man at Kings'—I might never have met him otherwise. And thank you much more for the wonderful Indian article. What a feeling Indians can have about goodness. They move towards it with a natural warmth. Whether I deserve such a tribute is another matter but I value it more than I can say—far more than the award of the American Professor from Swarthmore—on the same subject.

Also, old Mulk got a little—I thanked him/or the nice things he said to me, and the interesting things he said about me. A fair enough division. I am so glad his tribute was not cut.

With love and much gratitude,

Morgan

King's College
Cambridge

13 July 1967

Dear Natwar,

That news! Please accept my best congratulations and I hope I may have the pleasure of greeting you both in this country. Times are indeed difficult in your country (and in others) and one scarcely has anything to say, except sincere wishes for 20 August. I send you every good wish and my respectful greetings to your wife to be.

Morgan

C. Rajagopalachari
(1878–1972)

C. Rajagopalachari or Rajaji—who was also known as CR—was one of Gandhiji's prominent chelas *(followers). In 1927, the Mahatma nominated him as his successor. He changed his mind a decade later, and Rajaji's successor was Jawaharlal Nehru.*

C. Rajagopalachari possessed the sharpest mind among Gandhiji's followers. He was Premier of the Madras Presidency from 1937 to 1939. He ran his administration with exemplary efficiency. In 1942, he fell out with Gandhi. He was not in favour of the Quit India Movement. After Independence, he was Home Minister in Jawaharlal Nehru's Cabinet, Governor of West Bengal and finally succeeded Lord Mountbatten as the last Governor General of India. He became critical of Nehru's politics, and in 1959, launched the Swatantra Party as an alternative to the Congress. It did not last long; it could not.

C. Rajagopalachari came into my life accidently. He was 85 when he arrived in New York in October 1962. He was leading the Gandhi Peace Foundation delegation. The purpose of its visit was to persuade the United States to stop testing nuclear weapons. He met President John F. Kennedy, who, according to B.K. Nehru—our Ambassador in the USA—was impressed by CR's plea.

I was, at that time, posted to a permanent mission to the United Nations in New York. Normally, Rajaji would have been a guest of Ambassador B.N. Chakravarthy, who was heading our mission at the UN. However, his house was under repairs at the time. Therefore, I was asked to put up Rajaji in my spacious twin-bedroom apartment. This was his first ever visit abroad. Inevitably, I saw much of him and what I saw of the saintlike CR, I liked. I got the impression that he too liked me. He was over fifty years older than me.

His manners were impeccable, his speech gentle and soft. He was neither indifferent nor condescending. The fifty-page daily edition of The New York Times *baffled him. Most politicians (including me) are exceedingly fond of their voices. CR was free of verbosity.*

I had many discussions with him. One day, I said to him, 'Sir, Lord Mountbatten sold Partition to Panditji and Sardar Patel.' He replied, 'Now, let me tell you, I sold Partition to Mountbatten. I told him that partition was the only answer.'

I persisted by saying that Gandhiji was against Partition. 'Gandhi was a very great man but he saw what was going on. He was a very disillusioned man. When he realized that we were all for Partition, he said, "If you all agree, I will go along with you," and left Delhi the next day.'

After CR left New York, I naturally thought he would forget me. He did not, as these letters will show.

⁓

60, Bazlullah Road
Thyagaroyanagar
Madras 17

27 October 1962

My dear Natwar Singh,

I arrived here from Rome via Bombay and Delhi yesterday to receive a boisterous welcome at the airport in Madras. I shall never forget your kindness and your total surrender of your apartments to me. Convey to Swamy my heartfelt gratitude for all his attentions. I would not have returned well and hale and hearty but for his excellent service as my Nala and Bheema of the kitchen.

Yours sincerely,

C. Rajagopalachari

Shri K. Natwar Singh
First Secretary
Permanent Mission of India to the United Nations,
New York.

60, Bazlullah Road
Thyagaroyanagar
Madras 17

6 January 1963

My dear Natwar,

I wonder if you have really taken up the boring task of revising the translation of my stories and putting it on its legs, as I mercilessly suggested to you, instead of doing it myself as I should.

Anyway I send two stories rendered into English by someone else here which typescript will reach you by second class Airmail, one of which you may find easier to improve and use for your anthology.

Yours sincerely,

C. Rajagopalachari

(C. Rajagopalachari)

60, Bazlullah Road
Thyagaroyanagar
Madras 17.

10 December 1963

My dear Natwar Singh,

I am sending an unrevised and badly (English idiom) translated set of my short stories which is in the press and which I have asked to be thoroughly revised by one who is good in English idiom before publication. You may select any story or stories you choose for your anthology and improve the English. It may be wise to make the selection so as not to furnish matter for propaganda against unreformed India. (See enclosed letter from Bhartiya Vidya Bhawan, Executive Director.)

Do you think you can yourself improve this book of stories for me in respect of the English of it? Can you find the time and the patience? In that case you have to get the pages pasted on broad paper for entering the corrections. I fear you will not be able to undertake this labour of love. If you do it would be a memento of our happy friendship developed during the Kennedy era. What a tragedy of stupid crime this assassination!

Yours sincerely,

C. Rajagopalachari

(C. Rajagopalachari)

encl: 1
Sri K. Natwar Singh
New India House, 3 East 64th Street
New York.

60, Bazlullah Road
Thyagaroyanagar
Madras 17.

21 January 1964

My dear Natwar Singh,

I am glad you have taken over Hunchback Sundari.[1] Perhaps it is a little overweighed with Upanishad talk. But as you say it is Indian and therefore suitable for an anthology.

I believe Jawaharlal Nehru will soon be well. He is not likely to overwork now.

Yours affectionately,

C. Rajagopalachari

(C. Rajagopalachari)

Sri Natwar Singh
New York

---

[1]This story by Rajaji was included in his *Tales from Modern India*, published in 1964, in New York.

60, Bazlullah Road
Thyagaroyanagar
Madras 17.

28 February 1964

My dear Natwar Singh,

Thank you for sending me your beautiful Forster book. I have been glancing through it and also reading here and there. Of course I read all that you have contributed. Mr. Forster is a fascinating person. Narayana Menon's contribution is first class. Of course the many quotations from Forster himself are entrancing.

Thank you for honouring me with this beautiful book and writing the words you have written on the flyleaf.

Yours sincerely,

C. Rajagopalachari

(C. Rajagopalachari)

Shri Natwar Singh
New India House
3 East 64th Street
New York 21 (USA)

60 Bazlullah Road
Thyagaroyanagar
Madras-17

21 August 1965

My dear Natwar Singh,

It is some time since we exchanged letters. I trust you continue flourishing in the literary world in U.S.

I read Saturday Review, New York Times weekly, Progressive (Madison, Wisconsin) U.S. Report and World News, and the picture I gather from columns, editorial comments and cartoons is that President L.B. Johnson has the worst press ever for a President or a Prime Minister anywhere in the world. I admire the way in which he has held himself up and goes on.

I am sure you will contribute your bit to welcome Mrs. T. Sadasivam (M.S. Subbulakshmi)[,] the illustrious singer, who is going on invitation to the U.N. inauguration this year. You were so kind to me and my fellow delegates of the Gandhi Foundation when we were there. I can never forget your generosity and the beautiful food and attention I got in your apartments. Sri C.V. Narasimhan (of the U.N.) will look after Mr. and Mrs. Sadasivam and their musical group.

Yours sincerely,

C.Rajagopalachari

(C. Rajagopalachari)

Sri Natwar Singh
New India House,
3 East 64th Street
New York 21.

60, Bazlullah Road
Thyagaroyanagar
Madras 17.

31 August 1965

My dear Natwar,

It was so good of you to write and write so promptly. I have shown the letter to the Sadasivams and they are very grateful and look forward to meeting you.

I was glad to read what you write about President Johnson. It confirmed my own impression. But it is good to get a confirmation from one like you living in New York.

I have no influence on Fateh Singh[1]. Even Tara Singh[2] who is a very good friend would not listen to me if I asked him to give up any plan he had decided upon! I think something will be done by the Prime Minister to induce Fateh Singh to give up his fast.

Yours affectionately,

C. Rajagopalachari

(C. Rajagopalachari)

Sri K. Natwar Singh
New India House
3 East 64
New York 21, N.Y.

---

[1]Fateh Singh was an Akali leader who led the campaign for the establishment of a Punjabi Suba.
[2]Also Master Tara Singh, perhaps the most important Sikh leader.

60, Bazlullah Road
Thyagaroyanagar
Madras-17

16 September 1965

My dear Natwar Singh,

I was surprised to get a letter from you from Rajasthan and sorry to read the contents.[1] My sincere condolences to all of you. I hope this letter will reach your hands before you leave for New York. God bless you.

There are fire-eaters in Delhi even in this decade who believe India is strong enough to govern border people by force of arms and maintain the Indian Economy for grand plans besides normal administration. Our P.M. is in the hands of two groups—one guiding his foreign policy, another his internal policy, he himself only concerned in winning the next elections for the Congress. It is a tragedy that 460 millions of people are placed under charge of people whose knowledge of diplomacy is disgracefully below requirements just when the world has shrunk into a single puzzle.

Yours affectionately,

C. Rajgopalachari

(C. Rajagopalachari)

Shri Natwar Singh
Govind Niwas
Bharatpur
Rajasthan

---

[1] CR was referring to my father's demise on 7 September 1965.

Naoroji Road,
Kilpauk
Madras-10

6 March 1966

My dear Natwar Singh,

This is to tell you I read four reviews of the Stevenson books in Saturday Review in Jan 1. You have become a regular literary figure of the U.S. Good! And unlike our Indian authors who write 2nd to 3rd rate books for the US consumers, you write good stuff. Quite equal to what the best reviewers in the western journals write.

I noted your remarks about the striking difference between quotations and reviewers' language—what you have so well described as the "triumph of literature over journalism." I used to feel this and enjoy it since long ago....

Kind regards.
Yours affectionately,

C. Rajagopalachari

(C. Rajagopalachari)

C. Rajagopalachari
Naoroji Road,
Kilpauk
Madras-10.

1 April 1966

My dear Natwar Singh,

The enclosed letter was sent by me in the hope that the New York Times people would take it and forward it to Louis Fischer wherever he might be. But obviously the N.Y.T. people have other work to do.

Will you kindly take charge of this old letter and send it to Fischer to his correct present address which I am sure you know or will be able to find out. Your last letter was very pleasant reading. My best wishes to you. I feel you should settle down and become an American, with fond memories of India, unless the Government of India knows how to utilise your gifts and offers you a good place.

Yours sincerely,

C. Rajagopalachari

(C. Rajagopalachari)

encl: 1
Sri Natwar Singh
404 E, 66th Street
New York - 21
N.Y. (USA)

Naoroji Road
Kilpauk
Madras-10

14 May 1966

My dear Natwar Singh

Trust you have got reconciled to New Delhi between which and New York there is a whole world of difference. And particularly External Affairs atmosphere may be stifling.

I had a long meeting with the blind writer Ved Mehta who must be pretty well known to you. He filled the whole time with comprehensive questions he had ready, for me—all based on calumnies he had collected in advance!

With kind regards.

Yours sincerely,

C. Rajagopalachari

(C. Rajagopalachari)

Naoroji Road
Kilpauk
Madras-10.

20 May 1966

My dear Natwar,

I have your letter of May 18. I was glad to read it. It confirmed my own impression of Ved Mehta. I had feared I was guilty of an unfavourable prejudice, but your letter has cleared my conscience.

I am glad you are with the P.M. I am getting to have a very good opinion of her. God bless her. I feel like a father or grandfather-like to her.

Good luck to you.

Yours sincerely,

C. Rajagopalachari

(C. Rajagopalachari)

Naroji Road
Kilpauk
Madras-10.

24 November 1966

My dear Natwar,

I was so glad to read your letter of 22 November.

I shall indeed be very glad if you can get me the N.Y.T. review of your anthology. I have not yet received the copy of the book from the publishers. Sea mail takes more time.

I am not surprised you so much like the service under Smt. Indira Gandhi. She is splendidly endowed with all the graces of a good civilized lady. She grew up under the example of her gracious father.

I can never forget the moving gesture of her affection when she came and received my daughter at the Delhi railway station (Mrs Devadas Gandhi), when I took her to Delhi from Bombay after she unexpectedly and cruelly lost her husband. Indira Gandhi whom I did not expect was at the station and led my daughter to the car like a sister. The touch was a consolation both to her and to me. This was August 1957, when I had already begun openly and severely to criticise Jawaharlalji.

Yours sincerely,

C.Rajagopalachar

(C. Rajagopalachari)

Shri Natwar Singh
New Delhi

Naoroji Road,
Kilpauk
Madras-10.

9 January 1968

My dear Natwar,

Thank you for your letter. It is interesting to note your collection of stories going round the world. No. Italy showed no interest in me except that good Pope John made me feel blessed. He was so kind to me in 1962. So he died soon after.

The Tamil stamp gained by the incident as you write. Things work in paradoxes in this muddled world.

I finished 89 in December 1967 and I am running 90.

About the I.C.S. people, my experience was that the Englishmen were on the whole better than the Brown people, who suffered from an inferiority complex and overdid their arrogance.

Yours sincerely,

C. Rajagopalachari

(C. Rajagopalachari)

Sri K. Natwar Singh
New Delhi

Naoroji Road,
Kilpauk
Madras-10

20 January 1968

My dear Natwar,

In spite of my very deteriorated eyesight, owing to lenticular as well as vitreous opacity, because you wrote about E.M. Forster's *Passage to India*, I read his short stories and his *Passage*, and completed the latter book today.

I have a feeling Forster is one of De Quincey's tribe—an opium eater genius. This is my fancy or notion based on the extremely subjective manner of his writing. This is the first time I read this eminent writer. Of his short stories, I liked two. The *Passage to India* I plodded through, though the book has quite a lot of heavy idealized natural descriptions which with this writer is a mannerism. E.M. Forster is a liberal, one of the many British liberals who hold that the mistake of the British regime was only the arrogance of the officials. In Forster's book the Englishman and woman come off best, the Musulman next best. The Hindu who is really detested—his social customs and his religious practices—all included, comes off worst.

Without the Englishman, India under the Hindus will go to rack and ruin, that was what E.M. Forster, his hero Fielding and Englishmen were sure of.

Perhaps it has proved true?[1]

Yours affectionately,

C. Rajagopalachari

(C. Rajagopalachari)

---

[1]Here I don't agree with Rajaji. His understanding of Forster's writing was flawed.

Naoroji Road,
Kilpauk
Madras-10.

25 March 1968

My dear Natwar Singh,

I am sorry about your wife's illness. I hope you will see her well soon.

I have firmly resolved not to write or dictate any recollections or autobiography.

Yours affectionately,

C. Rajagopalachari

(C. Rajagopalachari)

Shri N. Natwar Singh
New Delhi

Naoroji Road,
Chetput
Madras-31

20 September 1969

My dear Natwar Singh,

Since I wrote to you last I have been able to get at all the *Hindustan Times* issues relating to your book. The fact is that though the *Hindustan Times* comes regularly to me along with other papers I do not keep a file of them.

I have read Mr. Kohli's review, your angry long letter about it and Mr. Kohli's rejoinder. You need not have taken any notice of Kohli's review but you have dealt with it in full detail.

I assure you that Mr. Kohli's review is not so important as to deserve so much attention. We may leave the matter at this. Your long letter has dealt with all aspects at full length. The *Hindustan Times*' present editor is a new hand.

Yours sincerely,

C. Rajagopalachari

(C. Rajagopalachari)

Sri Natwar Singh
11, Lodi Gardens
New Delhi

IV

Nirad C. Chaudhuri
(1897–1999)

In the summer of 1954, Nirad C. Chaudhuri wrote a highly critical article on E.M. Forster, in Encounter, a new literary monthly edited by Stephen Spender and Irving Kristol. I showed it to Forster. He wrote one or two light-hearted comments on the margin of the article.

Soon after my return to India in August 1954, I wrote an article on E.M. Forster for The Illustrated Weekly of India. Nirad Babu referred to it when we met for the first time at a dinner at St. Stephen's College, New Delhi. A day or two later, I received a letter from him. It was the first step to a friendship that would last for over four decades. We had our differences—I am an E.M. Forster fan; he, a Kipling admirer. His bias against Gandhi and Nehru, I found unacceptable. Regardless, The Autobiography of an Unknown Indian (1951) gripped me. It widened my intellectual horizon. The literary style and form of the book enthralled me. It made the unknown Indian widely known.

In 1970, he settled down in Oxford. In 1973, when I was posted to London, I asked Nirad Babu and Smt. Chaudhuri to have lunch at our house in Hampstead. We had not met for almost a decade. His financial situation was precarious. I did what I could to help.

In 1987, he submitted the second volume of his autobiography, Thy Hand, Great Anarch! to the well-known British publishing house, Chatto & Windus. They turned it down. Which publisher would risk accepting a thousand-page long book by an author whose name was not even a fading memory?

Later in the year, a delegation of leading British publishers arrived in Delhi. It was led by Graham Greene, a senior director at Chatto & Windus. I spoke to him of the shabby manner in which they had treated India's outstanding man of letters. Greene was not aware of the book being submitted to Chatto & Windus. On his return to London, he made sure that Thy Hand, Great Anarch! (1987) was published on Nirad C. Chaudhuri's ninetieth birthday.

I had a hand in Nirad Babu being awarded the honorary degree *of Doctor of Letters by Oxford University in 1988.[1]*

I met Nirad Babu for the last time a few months after the death of his wife. His final years were as lonely as they could be. He passed away in Oxford on 1 August 1999, at the age of 101 years.

∾

---

[1] I spoke to Roy Jenkins, a former Cabinet Minister and at the time, Chancellor of Oxford University.

3 August 1955

Dear Mr Natawar Singh,

I was very glad to have your letter, which reached me only yesterday (the 2nd), although it bears the date 29th.

I have been wanting to get in touch with you, but the heat had completely knocked me out, and I had been neglecting not only social duties but also my writing engagements.

I think your idea of meeting sometime next week is excellent. But if you want to hear about my experiences and see the menus, among other things, would it not be better to come over to my place, and have tea (afternoon or high, as you please) with us? Why not come over on Sunday? Or alternatively any other evening. Please let me know how you would like it to be arranged, and, of course, if you want to you may bring along a friend or two.

Mr. Forster and I had a very interesting conversation, and he was very kind and courteous. Hoping to hear from you soon.

Yours sincerely,

(Nirad C. Chaudhuri)

Natwar Singh Esq.

P. O. Building
Nicholson Road,
Delhi

15 February 1960

My dear Natawar Singh,

I am enclosing two invitation cards to Dhruva's photographic exhibition, one for you and the other for your friend Mr. Shankar Menon[1] (KPS's[2] son—I hope I am right). I have sent an invitation to your other friend by post, and given another to Shiamsundar Nath[3] by hand.

As I do not know Mr Shankar Menon's address will you kindly send it on to him?

I am also sending a hand-drawn poster, for display (if possible, and if possibly only with propriety on your part) at the Gymkhana Club. If not keep it with you for the present, and I shall bring it away later. If displayed, take it back to your room after the exhibition is over, for we would like to preserve it.

Of course, I am expecting you and your friends to come.

Yours sincerely,

(Nirad C. Chaudhuri)

---

[1] An IFS officer.
[2] K.P.S. Menon, Foreign Secretary.
[3] An IFS officer.

41 Harefields,
Oxford, OX2 8NS

7 March 1978

My dear Natwar Singh,

When your instructions about sending you the proofs of my book on Hinduism came it had not even gone to press. It was sent last month, and I am afraid I cannot expect the proofs to come before April or May. Let me know how I can send a bound copy to you conveniently. In the meanwhile, the TLS[1] has published a long extract (7000 words) from the introduction, which gives my general appraisement in rational terms of the character of Hinduism as a religion. There are, of course, many other things in the book. I wonder if you see the TLS. As the issue for Feb. 3 was a special Indian issue you may at least have seen it. You may have also heard about it.

Today I am writing with a self-seeking purpose, actually for my eldest son Dhruva. He works at present as Professor in the Institute of Mass Communications in Delhi. He is not very happy there, because he feels he has little opportunity to do artistic work there, being burdened with routine work. So he has applied for the post of lecturer in photography at the Evelyn Home College of Commerce and Applied Arts at Lusaka under the Dept. of Education and Vocational Training of the Govt. of Zambia. He has given as reference a Zambian and Mr. Ashok Mitra (formerly of the I.C.S.). He did not know about you, and I am asking on my own if you could offer yourself as reference. As his application has been sent off, and I came to know about it only yesterday,

---

[1] *The Times Literary Supplement*

I thought I might ask you to write to the College, and if possible recommend him. I shall also be greatly obliged if you could use whatever influence you have there. I assure you that I shall ask nothing from you than what you think of his qualifications. He will have to justify his selection by his own work. Please let me know what you can do. If you would rather not intervene I would accept that. But I think you would not object to be a reference as to character, etc.

I am writing a long article—to be published in 2 parts for Khushwant Singh[1], taking your remark on me as a peg. You have said that if I am regarded as an Anglophile that is my doing. I am going to explain in what way I am Anglophile or pro-British, and in what way my critics are Anglophile and patriotic. It will be huge fun. I am sure you get the I.W.I.[2] at Lusaka. If you do not I shall send you a clipping.

With all good wishes to you and your wife I remain,

Yours very sincerely,

(Nirad C. Chaudhuri)

K. Natwar Singh

---

[1]Editor of *The Illustrated Weekly of India.*
[2]*The Illustrated Weekly of India.*

20 Lethburg Road
Oxford, OX2 7AU

28 August 1984

Dear Raj-Kumariji,

I am writing this letter to tell you how strongly I feel over what I called and would always call the second Amritsar Massacre.[1] Indeed, it is worse than the first.

I am deeply disquieted by the forbodings of its long term effects. I have read Sikh history only too well not to feel like that.

In Bengal we used to read about Sikh guru Baba Nanak to the battle of Gujarat with immense admiration—only people in India ever fought—really fought and ethically fought for their independence.

Since then, living in Delhi, I have real opportunity for knowing more about the Sikhs as a community of religious, honest, honourable, and brave men. Taken all in all, I now look upon them as the most admirable community, commendable as human beings, least tainted with the faults which are to be found in the Hindu character.

I hope in the hour of sorrow and tribulation for your people, this expression of opinion from an old Hindu will give you some consolation.

Yours sincerely,

(Nirad C. Chaudhuri)

---

[1]He was referring to Operation Bluestar in 1984.

41 Harefields,
Oxford, OX2 8HG

My dear Natwar,

I have to ask your forgiveness for not replying to your letter before this. The money arrived just in time to save me from serious embarrassment, and it met only arrears. The situation is continuing, and though I have been assured that something might come next month: there is uncertainty. This comes not only in the way of work, but came also in the way of writing to you. I hope you will understand.

A new situation has arisen which affects this question of my return to India. If the worst comes to the worst here, I had planned to go back, even without finishing this book. But as things are, I have to see what this situation will be for me. In any case, I shall not be able to write, and so that position will be as bad in India as here—probably worse.

I have never seen a government in India which was as undistinguished as the one Mrs G.[1] formed. If you have seen an article by me in the Spectator you may have read that I expected a Ministry of External Affairs where English would be intelligible to the diplomats in Delhi—Even that has not come about. The article was in the special for Jan 12. I also wrote an article in TLS 30 Nov. Did you see it? A review will soon appear...

(Contd...)

---

[1]Mrs Indira Gandhi

Thank you again for relief in a desperate situation.[2]

Yours affectionately,

(Nirad C. Chaudhuri)

PS: What about you coming to Europe (2) Is Khushwant likely to be in London?...

---

[2]At the time, Nirad Babu was in serious financial difficulties and in a modest way, I helped him.

My dear Natwar,

I am enclosing the screed on your book. You may use it in any form you like, or get it published as a full-length review. I hope you will like it.

I might tell you privately that there are a number of bad misprints in it, and one which is the worst is on p. 34 in the line.

'The Jatni did not in vain bear the pain of *travel*,'

English printers have become so illiterate that they no longer know the word travail.

There is another point to which I would draw your attention. The index has Najib Khan and Najib ud-Daulah as if they were two different persons.

I might tell you that the picture (traditional portrait) of Surja Mal which you print was seen by me first when I was a schoolboy in a text-book of history published so far as I remember by Indian Macmillan. That was as far back as 1911 or 1912.

Last of all, I would thank you for giving me a copy of your book.

Let me also know what you thought of my latest article in the T. o I.

Yours very sincerely,

(Nirad C. Chaudhuri)

Kumar Natwar Singh

A review of K. Natwar Singh's book *Maharaja Suraj Mal,
1707-1763: His Life and Times* (1981) by Nirad C. Chaudhuri.

Nirad C. Chaudhuri,
41 Harefields, Oxford, OX2 8HG

This book is both a history and a *tarpana* (oblation) of
ancestors, for Kunwar (Kumara) Natwar-Singh (Natavara
Simha) belongs to the princely house founded by Suraj
Mal Jat. And he has written both as historian and as Son.
The subtitle *His Life and Times,* although conventional in
biographies, has perfect appositeness in this book, because
without the *times* in which Suraj Mal lived there would
have been no Suraj Mal to write about. It is perhaps true
of all countries, and is certainly true of India before the
British came, that political anarchy is the very condition
which allows exceptional individuals to achieve greatness
in politics. This view is supported by the fact that, since
independence in India, relatively stable political conditions
and utter personal mediocrity have remained closely
connected. Had Hindustan been in the eighteenth century
what it is today Suraj Mal would not have reached the status
even of a Bansi Lal. Natwar-Singh need not have quoted
Napoleon's saying: 'Circumstances! I create circumstances',
as a motto for his book. Before Napoleon Suraj Mal must
have thought in the same way, or, to be accurate, he must
have said: 'Circumstances! I create opportunities out of
circumstances'.

This book is important because it provides a particular
illustration of two general propositions about the social and
political life of India. The first of them is that political power

in the form of a dynastic kingdom could arise literally out of nothing. The second is that in the Hindu order the caste system has never suppressed any person who had genius.

As to the first proposition, I have written in my autobiography: 'The state became loose down to the last divisible cell, and sovereignty was reduced to the lowest denomination of political power; there was degeneration combined with negation. One unifying force, however, played on this world, but it was a wild and elemental force; it was the kingdom hunting urge of men of the soldier of fortune type.... They were the *nouveaux riches*, the parvenus, of power. Some of them even suggest the anthropologist's headhunters.'

As to the relationship between the Hindu caste system and the gifted individual's destiny, I have, in my *Continent of Circe*, quoted a remark of Elphinstone who came just in time to see the traditional Indian political system still at work. He wrote: 'The caste system has by no means so great an effect in obstructing the enterprise of individuals as European writers are apt to suppose. There is, indeed, scarcely any part of the world where changes of condition are so sudden and striking as in India.' The silly chatter against the caste system is the legacy of the British radical to the feeble Anglicized Hindu, and it has created a prejudice among the latter against declaring their proper surname, so that the son of a Madanlal Saxena now writes himself as Sudhir Lal.

When I wrote all that I had, of course, in mind men like Suraj Mal Jat as well as his Muslim opposite number and enemy, Najib ud-Daula, the Rohilla chief. Kunwar Natwar-Singh has illustrated the whole type of politics, which might paradoxically be called achievements in anarchy, in his short book, taking Suraj Mal as the protagonist in the drama. Anyone who wants to know what through the ages in India has made a man successful in politics should read this book, whereas any biography of Jawaharlal Nehru would mislead him, for Nehru was not born for India.

But the book is not simply about the Jats or even Suraj Mal. It is also a record of the achievements of the Jats under a typical Jat leadership. Apart from the great achievement of the creation of a Jat kingdom out of nothing, the Jats have three notable achievements to their credit. Two of them are in the military field—one in defeat: the defence of Mathura against Ahmad Shah Abdali, and the other in success: defence of Bharatpore against Lord Lake. And the third achievement is in the field of art—the building of the palace at Dig, one of the finest examples of architecture in India from the Mogul period. It is curious that when the architectural tradition of the Moguls was tending towards decay in the most important centres like Delhi and Lucknow, it was some minor Hindu chiefs who maintained its beauty unimpaired. And the chiefs were not only minor, they were also illiterate. In this field the Jat adventurer showed a taste rivalling that of an Italian Condottiere, but not shown by any Indian educated at Oxford and Cambridge. Natwar-Singh, I am glad to find, has not passed over this achievement of the Jats.

My Dear Natawar Singh,

Thank you very much for your letter and for the proof copy of your piece on me. I found it very interesting, and what you have written about E.M.F.'s review about my <u>Passage</u>[1] justifies my poor opinion of his character. He aired condescension towards me, which showed what a fool he was. But he was trying to square his account with me.

I follow different principles. I had an article ready pointing out what a poor novel his <u>Passage</u>[2] was, apart from his shoddy theme, it was full of howlers about Indian life. He made a Shudra the brother in law of a Brahmin (both Bengali) and gave the name of Amrit Rao to a Bangali barrister from Calcutta. But I never tried to publish it, because I hold that if I have personal relations of a satisfactory character with a man I don't criticise him unless it is a matter of duty.

Even when it is a duty, I don't criticise anyone if people might think that I have a personal reason to write unfavourably. The New York Review of Book offers me $500 to write a review of Ved Mehta's book on India. Since he was blind that book could not be authentic. But I told the editor that since V.M. had spread calumnies (all falsehoods) about me in his book, people might misunderstand me. I cannot understand how you could write favourably about his book on Gandhi. What can a potboiler (efficient) writing for an American public (who will never buy a book on India which is authentic)—and a Punjabi at that,

---

[1]Nirad C. Chaudhuri wrote *A Passage to England*, 1959, his reference to Forster's novel.
[2]E.M. Forster, *A Passage to India*, 1924.

understand about Gandhi—especially about his sexual obsession. G's sexuality is not to be understood in terms of the Kinsey Report, or the *Psychopathia Sexualis*. Hindu sensuality is of a brand and which is its own. When you read my book on Hinduism, you will get a glimpse of its real character and be startled.

You want an advance proof copy to read? If so, let me know if I can send it to you through the High Commission here. Though you come from Vrij[3], you do not know what Krishna of Vrij is.

You want to know what I think of Amita Malik's piece on me in the Times of India. Well, I am certainly flattered, but I also know what others write about me must be their image of me. I have readymade formulae to embody my view of other people's view of me. I am often asked: "We hear so many stories about you. Are they true?" I reply: "If they are for me, you should discount 95%, but if against, the whole 100%".

Yours very sincerely,

(Nirad C. Chaudhuri)

---

[3]Braj, as in the language of a region comprising Vrindavan, Gokul, Goverdhan and Barsana.

V

Lord Louis Mountbatten
(1900–1979)

He was the last Viceroy of India and her first Governor General. A close friend of Jawaharlal Nehru, Lord Mountbatten was diplomatically shrewd enough to be reverential to Mahatma Gandhi. For nearly four decades, Mountbatten's India record was looked upon as dazzling and more than stirring. He had mastered the art of self-promotion. However, the demythologization soon caught up. I should add, however, that he was always courteous to me.

In November 1973, Her Majesty Queen Elizabeth held a reception at Buckingham Palace for the Diplomatic Corps. Lord Mountbatten was also present there.

Mountbatten had known my wife's family since 1922, when he had come to India with the Prince of Wales, as his ADC. In 1974, Hem's father was Ambassador to Holland. On 18 June the same year, he was to leave for England to be the guest of Lord Mountbatten at his home—Broadlands—in Hampshire. On the 17th, he had even spoken to me at 12.30 p.m. when I returned to India House from an official lunch. Later, that very day, my secretary was to give me the shocking news that the Maharaja was no more. He had suddenly passed away due to a massive heart attack.

Mountbatten spoke to Hem, conveying his condolences. He also told her that he had informed the Queen.

In 1975, Mountbatten accompanied his grandnephew—Prince Charles—to India. As soon as he landed, Mountbatten called: 'Natwar, I hear Edwina and my portraits have been put in the basement of Rashtrapati Bhawan.' It took me time to convince him that the portraits were not in the basement. Such trivial things mattered to the charming and most handsome royal.

༈

Broadlands,
Romsey,
Hampshire.
SO5 9ZD

11 August 1965

Dear Sri Natwar Singh,

Thank you for your letter of 3rd August.

I am just off on a few weeks holiday but will refer your enquiry about an English Publisher to a former member of my staff to see what the possibility is and I will get in touch with you again on my return.

I saw Narendra Singh of Sarila[1] this morning on my way through London to France.

Yours sincerely

(Mountbatten of Burma)

---

[1]Permanent representative of India to the UN headquarters in Geneva.

16 June 1975

Dear Natwar,

When I saw you both at the end of the Lecture on Thursday I assumed you would both be coming along to the dinner at the Royal Automobile Club. I was extremely grieved to find that you had a previous engagement and would not be able to come.

I think I should explain that this dinner rather fell between two stools being partly organised in London by the IERE staff and partly by me at Broadlands.

I had given instructions that the same group of people should be invited this time as last time and had assumed that all would be well.

When, however, they sent the list to me [and] your names were not on it and I immediately rang up and drew their attention to this omission and told them to send an invitation to you at once.

I gather they did this but very late in the day and for this unintentioned discourtesy I must offer the apologies of the Nehru Memorial Trustees.

You have both been such splendid supporters of the Trust that your absence was deeply felt but we realised we had only our own inefficiency to thank for not having secured your attendance in time.

Once more, all my thanks to you both for the help you give.

Yours sincerely

Mountbatten of Burma

(Mountbatten of Burma)

28 June 1975

Dear Natwar Singh,

It is very kind of you both to send me greetings and felicitations on the occasion of my 75th birthday.

I appreciate this very much and also the kind thoughts in the second paragraph of your letter!

Yours sincerely

Mountbatten of Burma

(Mountbatten of Burma)

3 January 1976

Dear Natwar,

How nice of you both to send me a Greetings card which I much appreciated.

I have just written to the High Commissioner to say that I will be spending a night in Bombay in February flying between Jedda and Colombo.

With all best wishes to you both for 1976.

Yours sincerely

(Mountbatten of Burma)

Broadlands,
Romsey,
Hampshire.
SO5 9ZD.

5 August 1977

My dear Natwar,

Thank you so much for your letter of 6th July which arrived while I was on a visit to Kenya and I only saw it on the point of departure to spend the month of August at my place in Ireland, Classiebawn Castle. I am therefore dictating this reply to be typed and sent on to me for signature in Ireland.

I am so glad that you are now fully recovered from your nasty accident[1] and am delighted to hear of your appointment as Indian High Commissioner to Zambia and Botswana. I am only so sorry that my own travels prevented me having the chance of saying goodbye to you both in person but I want you to know how much I admire the splendid job you have done as Deputy High Commissioner in the United Kingdom. I am sure you will be equally successful in your important new appointment.

Thank you also for your kind remarks about the Jubilee. Throughout it has been a remarkable demonstration of loyalty and affection towards The Queen and indeed the whole of the Royal Family. Its success has surpassed all expectations.

---

[1] I had had a fall and had hurt myself.

With warmest best wishes to you both.

Yours sincerely

(Mountbatten of Burma)

28 August 1977

My dear Natwar,

I am writing to thank you for your letter of the 7th August which I have found on my return from a month's holiday at my place in Ireland, Classiebawn Castle, to which no mail was forwarded as my Private Office was closed down. The Estate Office merely sent out cards to say that no action could be taken.

This is about the only letter I can deal with during the 24 hours I am spending at Broadlands before taking some of my grandchildren out to Germany. If you would kindly ring up my Private Secretary, John Barratt, at this number he will see if there is any possibility of meeting you before you leave as of course I would like to see you very much if this is at all possible.

In all events I would like the opportunity of sending you my best wishes for your great appointment in Zambia.

Yours sincerely

(Mountbatten of Burma)

Broadlands,
Romsey,
Hampshire.
SO5 9ZD.

20 January 1978

My dear Natwar,

Thank you so much for your letter of the 5th January.

I have written to Sir Ian Gourlay who is our Chief Executive now at the International Office of the United World Colleges, and am asking him to send you a complete set of literature suitable for doing some propaganda to set up a United World Colleges National Committee in Zambia.

I realise that you will have to take the matter with President Kaunda[1] on a purely personal and informal basis to begin with but I will ask Sir Ian Gourlay to send you an exact report on the state of affairs in Nairobi, Egypt and Liberia and Senegal, to show that Africa is advancing very fast into the United World Colleges arena, particularly since the Lome Convention funds can now be given by the EEC to African countries to send boys and girls to the United World College of the Atlantic, St. Donat's Castle, in Wales.

I had no idea that Mac Mathai[2] could be such an absolute disloyal bounder and am quite horrified at what he has written.

(Contd...)

---

[1]Kenneth David Buchizya Kaunda, also known as KK, was the first President of Zambia.
[2]He was the private secretary to Jawaharlal Nehru, 1945–59.

I am making a speech at the Indo-British Association dinner at which I am taking the opportunity of putting the record straight without, I hope, appearing to defend myself too much. I will arrange for a copy of this speech to be sent to you, with the other literature by Sir Ian Gourlay when he writes.

With all best wishes to you both for 1978.

Yours sincerely

(Mountbatten of Burma)

14 February 1978

My dear Natwar,

Thank you so much for your letter of the 3rd February.

How nice of you to have talked to President Kaunda about the United World Colleges. In your letter you say "Sir Ian's material arrived just in time. K.K. was interested in the project. As I did not wish to add to his paper work I took the liberty of telling him that you would be writing to him. He was delighted."

This is slightly ambiguous to me because I am not sure whether you left behind the material which Ian Gourlay had given you, with the President, or whether you want me to send a new lot of material to the President. In any case, I imagine it is best not to worry him about this until shortly before his visit in the Summer, as then I can ask for an interview to discuss it all with him.

I can also discuss all this with the Prince of Wales who really is now in charge.

With best wishes to you and Hem.

Yours ever,

(Mountbatten of Burma)

PS

Since dictating the above I have had your second letter and have seen John Barratt and he tells me that he has already spoken to you on the telephone and is arranging for us to meet at my little house in London, 2 Kinnerton Street, SW1, on my return from Germany, either on the evening of 6th or the morning of 7th September.

I look forward very much to seeing you then.

7 August 1978

My dear Natwar,

Thank you so much for your letter of the 28th July which arrived as I was on the point of departure to spend the month of August at my place in Ireland, Classiebawn Castle. I am therefore dictating this reply to be typed and sent on to me for signature.

I am delighted to have a copy of your article on my old friend Rajaji and will read it with great interest. As a matter of fact I have just accepted an invitation to Chair the Rajaji Centenary Lecture to be given in London in December which is being organised by the Bharataya [Bharatiya] Vidya Bhavan.

As you will probably have heard, I had a most useful and interesting discussion with Dr. Kenneth Kaunda. He showed great interest in the United World Colleges project and gave instructions that his Ministers were to work out all the details for Zambia's participation. He also told his High Commissioner in London to visit Atlantic College at the first opportunity and she is in touch with the International Office. So all seems to be going well but it would be most helpful if you could also keep up the pressure from your end.

With very best wishes to you and your wife.

Yours ever,

(Mountbatten of Burma)

Broadlands,
Romsey,
Hampshire.
SO5 9ZD.

11 November 1978

My dear Natwar,

Thank you so much for your letter of the 2 November.

Many congratulations on the success of your article on Rajaji.

It was very kind of you to have talked to President Kaunda and I hope you will let me know what follow-up action he finally decides to take.

I invited Indira Gandhi to come down to Broadlands for lunch or dinner, like she used to in the old days with her father. I also offered to have her for tea or drinks at my little house in London.

There are only two official events in her honour, dinners on the 13th and 16th November. In both cases I have a genuine previous engagement as I was asked very late.

My personal friendship with all the Nehru family remains as ever, regardless of what she may have done during the Emergency.

I am so glad your mother-in-law, the Rajmata of Patiala, has been elected to Parliament. She will be a great addition to it.

With all best wishes to you and your family.

Yours ever,

(Mountbatten of Burma)

VI

Vijaya Lakshmi Pandit

(1900–1990)

❦

Courtesy: Wikimedia Commons/Ron Kroon

Vijaya Lakshmi Pandit was eleven years younger than her brother, Jawaharlal Nehru, and seven years older than her sister, Krishna Hutheesing. Her career was glittering, by my standards: She was the first woman minister in India (in Uttar Pradesh, during 1937–39); Indian Ambassador to the Soviet Union (1947–49) and the United States (1949–51); first woman to be President of the United Nations General Assembly (1953–54); High Commissioner to the United Kingdom (1954–61); Governor of Maharashtra (1962–64); and member of the Lok Sabha (1966–68). She published her autobiography, The Scope of Happiness: A Personal Memoir, in 1979.

I got to know Krishna Hutheesing in 1944. Her sons, Harsh and Ajit, were in Scindia School with me. My proximity to her was known to Vijaya Lakshmi and was not a recommendation: If you were friendly with one, you had to be against the other.

There was, for a while, some possibility of my going to London in 1960 as her private secretary. She turned me down.

On 12 August 1960, I received an extraordinary letter from Krishna Hutheesing. 'Natwar...my sister has played another foul trick on me and stabbed me in the back. I'm coming to Delhi on the 13th evening by plane...10:30 or something, with Raja [her husband], and am going to have it out once and for all with the PM...'

The 'stab in the back' was healed by Lal Bahadur Shastri. Jawaharlal Nehru avoided getting involved in the constant bickering of his sisters.

For the 1963 session of the UN General Assembly, the prime minister sent Vijaya Lakshmi Pandit to lead the Indian delegation. Bearing in mind the London episode, I did not look forward to her arrival. By the time, her youngest daughter, Rita Dhar, had become a close friend of mine. Her mother stayed in the fancy Carlyle Hotel on Madison Avenue. Rita took up residence with her mother. To my surprise, I was appointed secretary-cum-ADC to the leader of the delegation. Rita had not been idle. She, in a casual manner, told me, 'You will adore mummy.'

When I met Mrs Pandit, I kept madam-ing her. She snapped: 'Stop calling me madam. What do you call Betty (Krishna Hutheesing)?'

'Masi,' I said.

'You can call me Masi.'

That was that. It was smooth sailing from then onwards.

19 December 1963

My dear Natwar,

I had three hectic happy days in London and arrived here quite worn out. There is a terrific schedule all ready for me, so I have no chance to relax. No peace etc.......

I want you to know how very much I appreciate all your help during my stay in New York.

You had many burdens and bore them all with great good humour. I am most grateful. It was nice getting to know you and I hope to continue this pleasant process.

The news here is disturbing. The P.M. is, by all accounts very weary and under terrific pressure. He is expected here on Christmas Day and his schedule is enough to kill the strongest man. I wish something could be done to persuade him to let go.

My sister[1] and Raja[2] are both in Delhi and both very ill mentally and physically. It's all very sad.

I hope you can have some rest now the assembly is over. You deserve it.

With affectionate good wishes,

Nan

(Vijaya Lakshmi Pandit)

---

[1]Krishna Hutheesing
[2]Raja Hutheesing, husband of Krishna Hutheesing.

21 January 1964

My dear Natwar,

I read the write up of the Forster book with pride and pleasure. I have also read the book and think you have done a good job...

Your letter of the 12th reached me today on my return from Bangalore. I was glad to have the clippings.

Ever since I came home from the U.S. I have been worried sick about the P.M.'s health. He looked so ill I could hardly bear to look at him. It was obvious he was heading for a breakdown and was driving himself mercilessly in spite of it. He was alone in the house due to Indu's absence and though he was accompanied by a doctor on his tour this poor little man was so junior, he literally trembles every time he had to approach P.M. There was no question of advice or assistance.

The day P.M and Indira left for Bhuvaneshwar I could have wept. He got up at 5.00 a.m after a late night & left at 6.45 a.m. going straight on from Bhuvaneshwar by helicopter—a rattling broken down affair to some other place for a perfectly silly engagement. After that there were meetings of the A.I.C.C. Next morning he couldn't get up. The doctor call this a Spasm—momentarily for a few hours he was not able to use his left foot and hand but by the night this righted itself. His blood pressure was terrifically high and he had to be put to bed. Fortunately, good doctors were instantly available. The journey back to Delhi did not tire him unduly and he is now looked after by a panel of doctors. There are resident nurses and a masseur. I was in Delhi for four days and was glad to find that visitors were not allowed except for two minutes and only about two a day. The press reports on this are not correct. I think the people themselves told waiting pressmen that they had spent half an hour with the P.M. to show their importance! What a world.

The problem now is going to be how to restrain Bhai. You know his sense of responsibility and the way in which he wants to take everybody's mistakes on himself—this obviously, must stop. He is required for a long time and must be made to understand it.

The Indian doctor is not firm and also sometimes frightened to annoy a big person. Indira is swayed in all sorts of directions and gives in. I do not quite know who is to take care of this precious life. As you know I am somewhat of a *persona nongrata*. One can but pray.

Delhi is a seething hive of intrigue. I sometimes wonder whether we are more prone to intrigue than others or if we are just more crude at the game. Even today we do not understand the vital need to work for the common good. Personal interests are the motivating force behind many 'leaders'.

I feel so helpless having to watch things happening which could be averted or better canalised—but for some unknown reason a door has been closed on me. Oh well—one must not complain. I certainly have had a good innings.

The Kashmir and Calcutta troubles must have made sad reading abroad.

Both were the results of actions by Pak supporters. This however does not lessen our responsibility. Only one good thing emerged from the holocaust that was the way in which both Hindus and Muslims joined together to attack the Bakshi[1] regime.

---

[1] Ghulam Mohammad Bakshi, Chief Minister of Jammu and Kashmir after Sheikh Abdullah.

It is to be hoped the government will take a firm stand in Kashmir now. This morning's papers say Bhutto is again raising the issue in the U.N.

In Bombay there is a storm over prohibition. Our Chief Minister has been courageous enough to ask for a gradual withdrawal and Morarji Bhai is behaving as if it were a matter of the highest morality and is challenging all and sundry to give him power and see what he can do.

Do keep in touch with me.

Affectionately,

Lucki

(Vijaya Lakshmi Pandit)

P.S.: My sister says she is going to the States in a few weeks. I don't know why. Rajan[2] leaves for her lecture tour on the 28th and will be away until April. Indira is going for the world fair.

The question of my Africa tour is hanging in the balance pending the appointment or otherwise of a foreign minister.

VLP

---

[3]Rajan Nehru, wife of R.K. Nehru, ICS, Secretary General, Ministry of External Affairs and Ambassador to China and Egypt.

Raj Bhavan,
Bombay

18 May 1964

My dear Natwar,

I have been meaning to write to you for some time but life has a habit of becoming confused and one is constantly involved in time-consuming activities that pay no dividends. At the end of the day, I am conscious of many wasted hours and yet I have not been unoccupied a single minute. This is the answer to your question as to why I wish to leave this post.

The people who drafted our Constitution naturally could not think of everything at that moment of elation. Cutting the Governor's powers to a certain extent was a good thing, but making the Governor into a mere figurehead has reduced the value of the post. I was not cut out to be 'The Hostess with the Mostess'. It is becoming meaningless and boring.

I have been advised to stand for Parliament and this appeals to me. There is no seat available at the moment as I do not wish to go to the Rajya Sabha but probably something will materialise in the course of the next few months.

When I was in Delhi three weeks ago, a rough itinerary for my visit to West Africa was being drawn up. I am supposed to attend a meeting of the Dag Hammarskjold[1] Foundation in Stockholm on the 23/24 June and the African visit was to be linked up with this. However, in the usual manner of our Ministry, no final letter has come to me and I am wondering if they want me to go at all. I had asked that you should be permitted to accompany me

---

[1] Swedish Statesman; Secretary General, United Nations, 1953–61.

on the ground that you were dealing with Africa and this would be a valuable experience for you.

I like your idea of attending the Security Council Debate on Apartheid and will get in touch with the P.M. Unfortunately, your letter arrived just after he had left. It seems natural that I should be associated with this Debate but the thinking of the Government does not always coincide with mine.

The A.I.C.C. is just over and I must say it was conducted in a more businesslike fashion than I had hoped. Speeches were good and to the point and the Prime Minister spoke on two occasions firmly and well. His main difficulty now is getting around as his left leg is weak and I doubt if it will get much better. But for this he has improved and one hopes that this progress will continue if he is careful to take sufficient rest.

The burning topic of the day in India is Sheikh Abdullah's release and passions are deeply involved. So far, he has merely been letting off steam and I suppose this is natural after a decade's incarceration. I wonder what tune he will play on his return from Pakistan. Except for the Swatantra Party—and even they are not unanimous on this point—the whole of India is united in pressing the Prime Minister not to give way on the matter of Kashmir's accession. The new Prime Minister, Sadiq[2], had lunch with me today. He is a quiet little man, but firm and, I think, as well able to handle this intricate business as anyone else in Kashmir. One thing in his favour is that he does not talk.

I met Rajan briefly in Delhi. She was full of the success of her tour and ready almost to start on a new one!

(Contd...)

---

[2]Sadiq Saheb was in fact the Chief Minister of Jammu and Kashmir.
[3]Wife of Krishna Hutheesing's younger son, Ajit.

The Hutheesings are as usual—sometimes up and sometimes down. Amrita[3] is still waiting for her baby which is expected in July. I will write again as soon as there from Delhi.

Affectionately,

Vijaya Lakshmi Pandit

(Vijaya Lakshmi Pandit)

Raj Bhavan,
Bombay

23 May 1964

My dear Natwar,

Letter from the ministry says you are too busy with the committee of 24 to accompany me on the West Africa tour but 'some other officer can be given this assignment'.

Let me know at once what you feel and whether you could leave New York between 10th July to the end of the month.

Could you also let me know the likely dates of the Security Council debate on apartheid.

In haste, affectionately,

Vijaya Lakshmi Pandit

(Vijaya Lakshmi Pandit)

23 June 1964

My dear Natwar,

Thank you for sharing our sorrow.[1] The tears of his beloved India and indeed the world have been ample evidence of his place in the hearts of his fellow-men.

You are so right when you say he was the most beautiful man in the world. Every action, every thought was beautiful and one cannot but be thankful that he died as he wished, in harness and in peace. In death the radiance and serenity of his face were quite extraordinary. We have much to live up to but I dare to believe the seeds he planted will bear fruit.

I will write more later. This is merely to send you my love.

(Vijaya Lakshmi Pandit)

(Vijaya Lakshmi Pandit)

---

[1]Vijaya Lakshmi Pandit is referring to the death of her brother, Jawaharlal Nehru. He passed away on 27 May 1964.

New Delhi

7 April 1965

My dear Natwar,

Thank you for your letter. Ever since I returned from the States I have been in trouble. First, I had a hemorrhage and then later when this was healing I developed a very bad sinus trouble, then again pulled through this time. I went to Parliament because I was determined to get reacquainted with procedures and people. My speech has brought so much criticism but I had to say what I said when I said it and all things considered I think it has shaken everyone out of the lethargy. Let me know your views about this!

Regarding the book it has been held up because some parts had to be re-written and I did not have the time. I am, however, going to work at it hard so that it may be completed in a few weeks. I will get in touch with you later.

I was sorry to hear that you had been ill again. This is quite unpardonable for a person of your age. Please look after yourself.

I will write at length later.

Yours affectionately,

Nan

(Vijaya Lakshmi Pandit)

24 January 1966

My dear Natwar,

So the world's largest democracy has chosen a woman to lead! Indu's election has made history—I hope and pray she may be given the <u>wisdom</u>. At present the nation is jubilant but when the first excitement wears off the usual criticism and fault finding will begin. It is then that she must be tolerant and have safe counsel.

The air is thick with rumour about the new cabinet and the names will be known to you long before you receive this letter. I do not know who Indu's confidants are, except of course, Uma Shankar Dikshit[1] who has been Eminance Grise for many years. But whoever advises I hope for the sake of the country the advice is just and sound.

We are facing a crisis of great magnitude, not only matters like food, Tashkent, etc., but the physiological crisis which has us in its grips and needs the full hand and far seeing vision of a real leader._____

26th. I was interrupted and now the new Government is in power. A definitely rightwing government and one over which the establishment will have some control. I hope Indu gets cooperation and support.

---

[1]Closely associated with the Nehru family for decades; was Cabinet Minister and Governor of Karnataka.

The manner in which the world has hailed the election has been most heart warming.

This is the stranger letter—do forgive me. I am now in Bombay helping Tara to move into her flat. I shall return in time for parliament.

Write when opportunity offers.

Love and good wishes,

Nan

(Vijaya Lakshmi Pandit)

181-B Rajpur Road
Dehradun-248009

11 February 1984

My dear Natwar,

On the 27 Jan I had written to tell you how happy I was to know you had been awarded the Padma Bhushan. I do not think the letter reached you because four others posted at the same time seem to have miscarried.

I am writing again just to repeat my congratulations—to send you my love—

As always

Vijaya Lakshmi Pandit

(Vijaya Lakshmi Pandit)

VII

Mulk Raj Anand
(1905–2004)

Mulk Raj Anand was born in Peshawar (now in Pakistan), in 1905. His family did business in copper and silver items. His father joined the British Indian Army and rose to be a Havaldar. His mother was from a peasant family in central Punjab.

One of the contributors to my book on tributes on E.M. Forster[1] was Mulk Raj Anand. Although we met at Narayan Menon's flat in Wellesley Road, New Delhi, we had been corresponding for several years before that.

Fame had not come easily to him. His first novel, Untouchable, was turned down by nineteen publishers. (He had told me he was seriously considering suicide.) Mulk was then studying in London. He sent the manuscript to E.M. Forster, whose foreword to the book made its publication possible.

Mulk was fun to be with. He wrote too much; he led a disorganized life. He was a loyal friend, warm-hearted and prone to being easily taken in. He cared little for money. His friends included Jawaharlal Nehru, Indira Gandhi and George Orwell.

A more un-Gandhian individual than one could ever come across, yet he deeply admired the Mahatma. He had even spent a few weeks at Gandhiji's ashram in Sabarmati. Mulk shed his Marxism late in life. He spent the last years of his life in Lonavla in Maharashtra. Before I could visit him, he passed away at the age of 99.

ॐ

---

[1] K. Natwar Singh ed., *E.M. Forster: A Tribute*, Harcourt, Brace & World, 1964.

F 20 University Campus
Chandigarh–3
(India)

29 March 1963

My dear Friend,

I have your kind letter of 19th March. I vividly remember our meeting at the house of Narayan Menon. I only wish I have been able to see you for pure friendship after that. But my visits to Delhi are always rushed and there was no occasion to ask Narayan whether you were still there or have gone abroad. I hope if you return here for little while, that we will meet.

As you know, my old ties with E.M. Forster are very dear to me. I have learnt much from this Guru. And, of course, I would like to contribute a short piece of reminiscences and comments to the volume which you are envisaging. I hope to send you this piece before the 25th of May.

Please give my warm regards to Raja Rao and Shanta Rama Rau. Please tell Shanta not to despise me as much, as she does. I have tried to serve our country as intensely as I could. If I have failed she could tell me why I have failed, but not dismiss me out of hand, merely because of political differences. Raja Rao and I also have political differences, but I have the highest respect for him and, I believe, he has no contempt for me.

(Contd...)

145

In literary criticism a battle of ideas is permissable, but not mere dismissal of an old writer with a phrase.

With kindliest wishes,

Yours sincerely,

Mulkaj·Anad

(Mulk Raj Anand)
Tagore Professor
Art & Literature

Shri K. Natwar Singh,
404 East 66 St.
New York 21, N.Y.

25 Cuffe Parade,
Colaba,
Bombay 5.

8 May 1963

My dear friend,

I was thinking of you and had infact written a piece for the Souvenir volume for Morgan Forster, only last week end. It is in form of a letter, because I found I could say things more simply and directly than in any other kind of narrative. Reminiscences would become too long. And criticism would be invidious in a volume of this kind. Gratitude is best expressed in a direct approach, specially, as some asides are also possible. I will revise this letter and send it to you by the middle of this month.

I am afraid, I have lost touch with Ahmed Ali a long time ago, and I do not know his present whereabouts. Perhaps, the Pakistan Foreign Office would redirect the letter.

Please give my very warm regards to Dorothy Norman[1] and tell her I shall write to her soon. As you probably know, my duties in Chandigarh are onerous enough. And now I have come after a really two months tour of the monuments of middle India and the Deccan to try to prepare three numbers of MARG[2] ahead.

Incidentally, may I impose on you, on behalf of MARG and ask if you can send me a list of say about fifty people, libraries and individuals in America, who might wish to subscribe to

(Contd...)

---

[1] A friend of Jawaharlal Nehru and Indira Gandhi.
[2] An Indian art magazine founded by Mulk Raj Anand.

MARG. I am afraid we are unable to break through via the book sellers, because, after all, it is a specialist magazine and not exactly popular. The Prime Minister buys 500 copies for the Embassies and I don't know if you ever see it. I do not wish you to waste your time on this list immediately, but perhaps you can send this to me in the course of next two months.

With kindliest wishes,

Yours sincerely,

Mulk Raj Anand

(Mulk Raj Anand)

Shri K. Natwar Singh,
404 East 66th St.,
New York, 21. N.Y.

34–38 Bank Street
Bombay
Telephone: 252576

22 May 1963

My dear friend,

I am grateful for your most nice letter of 14th May. I think my own second note has crossed yours.

I am sending you a draft to my Homage to E.M. Forster. Perhaps between now and the time the book goes to press, I may think of a paragraph or two to add to this letter.

The personal list of friends you have promised for Marg will be gratefully received, as I am sure there are quite a few people in America in the Universities whose interests in India are deeper than those of the average novel reader.

With kindliest wishes,

Yours sincerely,

Mulk Raj Anand

(Mulk Raj Anand)

Shri K. Natwar Singh,
Apartment 9-E,
404 East 66th Street,
New York 21,
New York
U.S.A.

Department of Fine Arts
University of Punjab
Chandigarh-3.

13 August 1963

My dear Friend,

I am grateful for your courtesy in sending me the typescript of my letter to Morgan Forster. I have added a few things here and there in the attempt to suggest all those many things which were left out. Of course, I shall have failed to communicate even now the exact shade of my feelings towards this great man, because he is so human, so much more human than most people. I particularly wanted to draw attention to some of his weaknesses, which make him difficult and yet lovable. Anyhow, such an attempt can only be made in a longer piece. But, perhaps, even that will be misunderstood. People have forgotten that to do homage to genius one must also record the failings of a genius, without viciousness and anger.

With kindliest wishes,

Yours sincerely,

Mulk Raj Anand

(Mulk Raj Anand)

Shri K. Natwar Singh
Apt. 9-E, 404 E 66th St.
New York

Enc: Letter to E.M. Forster

PS: In case you can't read my scrawl, I attach slip for main addendum on p 3.

Department of Fine Arts
University of Punjab
Chandigarh-3.

17 March 1964

My dear Friend,

This is to thank you for your welcome news of March 9th. I wrote to you about ten days ago asking for a copy of the book. Perhaps that letter has crossed this one of yours.

I was rather moved at the end of the last year when I received a letter from Morgan Forster, in his old whimsical style. And it reassures me to know that he has not at taken umbrage at my open letter.

I hear well of the book from Krishna Kripalani[1] and Raja Rao, whom I met in Delhi two days ago. I am sanguine that the special circumstances which bind us to E.M. Forster will be appreciated by many people. You did well in sensing the situation when you decided to bring out the volume.

Please send me the royalties due to me any time you like. If you do so before the 10th of April, then please send it to my Panjab University address, otherwise 25 Cuffe Parade, Bombay will find me until the end of June.

With kindliest wishes,

Yours sincerely,

Mulk Raj Anand

(Mulk Raj Anand)

---

[1]Secretary of the Sahitya Akademi.

12 November 1964

My dear friend,

I wish we could be as efficient here as you are in New York. Unfortunately, I had no help in the office for a whole month, due to the vagaries of the University. That is why I could not answer your letter of October 9 promptly. Even now it is going to be a brief and perfunctory to your questionnaire:

i) Date, place and year of birth: 12-12-1905, Peshawar N.W.F.P.
ii) Family background:
    His father came from the silver and coppersmith craft but joined the British Indian Army; his mother was a peasant woman from Central Punjab. Anand was apprentice to the crafts and also live in the villages hearing folk ballets [sic] and tales of the people.
iii) Education: School, College, University attended. Badly educated in the schools and colleges of Punjab; made up some arrears of understanding while researching for Doctor's Degree in Philosophy in University College, London and in Cambridge.
iv) When and why you decided to become a writer?
    The death of a cousin, who was 9 years old, when Anand was eleven, shocked him into asking fundamental questions about life. Later he came under the influence of the Poet Iqbal and began to write adolescent works in Hindustani.

Exiled in London, he was disillusioned with his education. In North Wales, he wrote a confession of 2000 pages. This became the source book for all his writings, which were compelled by the need to communicate the agony of his generation and the attempt at compassion.

v) Which Indian and foreign authorities have impressed or influenced you?

Tagore, Iqbal, Tolstoy, Gorki, Forster, Malraux, Celine, Miller (Henry), Luhsun...

vi) What in your view is the major achievement of Modern Indian Literature?

Synthesis of Western and Indian Values resulting in renascent efforts towards the making of a 'modern' sensibility and consciousness.

vii) Do you think that the English language has a future as far as modern Indian literature is concerned?

I think communication born of compulsion, to establish solidarity among human beings, and to confront one's destiny, is possible in any language. Poetry is however, difficult in a foreign language because it is intimately bound up with kinetic imagery and the metabolism which has local affiliations in speech. But prose depends on direct communication as well as suggestions and inner urges; so it is possible for anyone to learn and speak in a foreign language. The English language has become integral to the Indian imagination, as did Persian at one time. In the present state of world shrinking, the English language will be written in India for ever. Therefore, some literature may arise.

viii)Your views, in brief, on the future of modern Indian literature.

If the intelligentsia of India achieve 'modern' consciousness, which means the illumination of the renaissance in the arts and sciences, the Indian sensibility may be renewed. Then the writers could pick up some flowers from the Himalayas of their tradition and also absorb the flowers from the alps and write significant works from the fragrance of the bouquet. In that case, there is a future from Modern Indian Literature.

ix) What are the problems facing the Indian writer today? Poverty, ignorance, humiliation, self-disgust, guilt, the weight of the past and the difficulty of knowing the contemporary situation of the world.

x) Names and dates of publications of your books: Untouchable, 1935; Coolie, 1936; Two Leaves and a Bud, 1937; The Village, 1939; Across The Black Waters, 1940; The Sword And the Sickle, 1942; The Barbers Trade Union, 1943; The Big Heart, 1944; Seven Summers, 1948; Private Life of an Indian Prince, 1951, etc. etc.

Yours

(Mulk Raj Anand)

8 January 1975

My dear friend,

I happened to be shooting the little film on Krishna as a naughty boy, near the Surkuti by the Jumna during the last week of December. After the rigours of this work (may the gods who are not there, spare you the humiliation of ever doing a film in India!) I thought of going to Jaipur to find out some books which may help me to understand how Swai Jai Singh managed to survive for 43 years on the Gaddi of Jaipur, how he could keep the Maharatta empires at bay and the king makers of Delhi away from his doors, as also how he could build up Indian astronomy in twenty years. My brakes failed in Agra, so we rested the night at Bharatpur and naturally, I was reminded of you, much more intensely because, we met your cousin, Shri Ragunath Singh, who lives in the big haveli in the middle of the vast farm. As was to be expected, his cordial hospitality made me want to go back again as soon as possible and there is a bird sanctuary which I love.

I was able to photograph the Observatory in Jaipur and sundry other things. Then, by sheer coincidence, I had a call from Bhopal about something on which I have been working for years—Sanchi. And there I met again the very sincere, young doctor of Philosophy, who has a thesis on 'E.M. Forster in India', has compiled many of the letters from Morgan to unknown friends (I mean unknown to us). I had mentioned him to you when I met you in London and I had asked you, on his behalf, for permission to reproduce Morgan's letters to you, published in the <u>New Statesman</u>. You had nodded assent and I hope that you can now put this on paper. Also, could you send me by air freight type-script of the letters or a copy of the <u>Statesman</u>.

Dr. Hamid Hussain wants you also to give him permission for your major article on Morgan Forster for his Anthology. About this he will write to you himself later.

Apart from Morgan, I hope, perhaps through him, we share certain things. These I would like to go on sharing with you, which means that you might write to me what you are doing away from your exalted position. And if you come home, please let us spend some time together just to be with each other to talk at random.

I would like to go on with this note and gossip, but as I have just come back after a month of being away, there are the inevitable arrears of MARG work.

May I wish you, Hem and the children a good New Year.

Yours,

Mulak-Raj

(Mulk Raj Anand)

H.E. Shri Natwar Singh
Deputy High Commissioner of India,
India House,
Aldwych,
London W.C. 2.

My dear friend,

I have just come back from a MARG research tour of Karnatak and Tamilnadu and am full of the euphoria of the beauties and spendours and glories I have seen in the ancient monuments.

By chance, however, I happened to see a film called *Kissa Kursi Ka* in Bangalore. You may know that this is a much talked of new version of the old film which Sanjay & Co. destroyed. It is an extravaganza in black and white rather simplified with some good satire in it. I thought it is atypical vulgar Hindi film. But on the next morning, I read the newspapers and found that what Mrs. G is doing on the platforms of South India at the moment, surrounded by all the hoodlums, and aya-Rams and Gaya-Rams, is more crude even than the film portrays. Somehow, anything goes. The Janata Government is not less distinguished in its horse trading. And the whole atmosphere seems utterly immoral. All the values which the great Jawaharlal stood [for], have gone by the board. It is not democracy but mobocracy.

I recalled to my mind all the time what Kamaladevi Chattopadhya said to me a few months ago, when I asked her about her health: 'I wish Mulk Raj I had died two years ago.'

Our dear Natwar, I can imagine how difficult it must have been for you to see the downfall of someone who served so loyally as a Secretary. You remember what hopes we had. And I vividly recall her strictures about me when she felt that I was backing the unscrupulous Krishan Khanna. How she could lose her sense of values I don't know...

I hope you will come via Bombay and stay with me for a day on your way north, because I am going to the Coomaraswamy seminar in Mysore University in early March. Then to the coastal area in Andhra for a model village I am trying to get sponsored for the Kalamkari workers. I may come to Delhi for Holi to contact the architects etc. and see you in the north if you are unable to break your journey in Bombay.

I think like all of us, you will have to forget the humiliations which have accrued to us because we did back the emergency even though half-heartedly. Do you remember coming to see me on your way to Office in London at Bill Archer's house, and how unhappy you were about the article written by the English member of Parliament called Abbey, about the experiences he had at the hands of the secret police at Ashoka Hotel. You were so sad that when later, Marilyn Silverstone came to photograph me, I could not melt my face into a smile and the photos all appeared later as images of a morbidly unhappy person.

In the agony of our minds, however, I would like you to have one consolation which I know is already there. Your love of literature.

And the second wonderful thing which will keep us going is the confirmation some of us have from Morgan Forster of the belief in friendship. And I have found ultimately, the third thing in our background which appeases all guilt, is the ability to create a whole day, every day, for ourselves through our work.

I know that these may seem like platitudes to you, but just at this time, these ideas seem to have acquired depth so far as I am concerned.

(Contd...)

This brings you and the family my very warm regards and please do not go away without seeing me.

Yours sincerely,

Mulk Raj Anand

(Mulk Raj Anand)

His Excellency,
Shri Natwar Singh,
High Commissioner of India, LUSAKA

34–38 Bank Street
Bombay
Telephone: 252576

Ref: Ed/393/87.   26 May 1978

My dear Natwar,

Of course I was most disappointed not to be able to embrace you during your visit home in India.

I am amenable to your suggestion of taking no royalty for the Indian edition of the book of Tributes to E.M. Forster.

Please mention somewhere in your notes that Mulk Raj Anand has been given the E.M. Forster literary award by Arnold Heinemann for his novel: *Confession of a Lover.*

I feel more proud of this award since it is connected with the name of our dear friend, guide and philosopher than even of the Sahitya Akademi award for *Morning Face.*

Only you never reviewed this book and perhaps you didn't even read it. I beg you to persist and say what you feel about it, since it was an ambitious effort of mine which quite a few people thought came out.

This brings you my warm regards from the cool of Khandala heights.

Yours sincerely,

(Mulk Raj Anand)

10 August 1978

My dear friend,

I have been involved in the new MARG policy to accompany each issue with a festival of the performing arts and an exhibition as well. This has put up our sales from 3,000 to 7,000. And I want to have the transition to stability by giving mere time to this labour of love, than to my writing. I wish I had not wasted five years being bogus Chairman of the Academy of Art, and had finished my long novel.

I am getting Firbank's FORSTER for review, but if you have his address, I would like to write to him and send him the one letter which Morgan wrote to me after reading my piece in your book.

Under your advice, I have sent a copy of the same to Dinanath Malhotra, suggesting he put it at the end of my piece, where I think it might go more appropriately than elsewhere.

You will be amused to know that Sardar Khushwant Singh goes from success to success, because the bitch goddess favours him! It seems, however, that he was literally ejected from his chair in the Weekly and put out of the office by the peons, because he did not want to take notice of the employers' polite notice to quit. Of course, they were equally crooked and had indulged him because he got them out of their prolonged suspense about the misappropriations. And the latest about him is that dear old Chelapathi Rao has written a letter to the Board of Directors of *National Herald* bitterly complaining that they might have consulted the Editor in Chief,—which means Chelapathi Rao—before appointing the new Editor. It seems, however, that Sardar Khushwant Singh had demanded that Chelapathi Rao should go before he would join as Editor of *National Herald* and Madame seems to have discarded the old loyal Nehruite for this skunk merely because he has turned *chamcha* to Sanjay Gandhi and Maneka. The devaluation of the currency of values is complete. The new Government is torn up by the squabbles of the leadership and Mrs G. is likely to come back within a year if things go on at the present pace of disintegration.

I would genuinely like to have your opinion of the 'Lover,' because if you do not think it is too bad, I will go on with the sequels with good heart.

I don't know why the British Council has not written to you when I suggested to them, on their approach to me, that you were the proper man for the seminar-to-be in Hyderabad. I will write, again.

Meanwhile, I feel that if you have time, you must make your article on Surajmal into a 100-page biography.

Do let's keep in touch.

Love,

Yours,

(Mulk Raj Anand)

His Excellency,
Shri Natwar Singh,
Ambassador of India,
LUSAKA. (Zambia)

25 Cuffe Parade,
Bombay 400005.

14 April 1982

My dear friend,

I was heartened to see in the papers that you have come home and will be in the South Block in-charge of policies.

Apart from the pleasure of knowing that you are back and the hope of seeing you, I wish to consult you in your official capacity about a convention of 51 world intellectuals which some of us are projecting to take place in Srinagar or Chandigarh on the theme: Jawaharlal Nehru's slogan: A Hundred Years of Peace—which means no war ever.

I have already seen Shri Sathe, Secretary, Ministry of External Affairs about this and would benefit from your advice in view of your intimate experience of foreign policies.

Our convention has been inspired by the initiatives taken by the Prime Minister and the Minister of External Affairs. Shrimati Indira Gandhi has encouraged us and though independent in our approach, we are naturally coincident with national policies.

Among those who are supporting this project are Sarvashiri G. Parthasarthy, P.N. Haksar, T.N. Kaul, B.K. Nehru, Prof. George Wald and Prof. Linus Pauling.

With warm regards,

Yours sincerely,

(Mulk Raj Anand)

PS: I am in Delhi for ten days.

4 July 1983

Dear friend,

Greetings!

This concerns a possible book for inclusion in the <u>dossier</u> for the Commonwealth Conference in November this year.

I was asked to advise on a beautiful album on India, especially for presentation to delegates of the coming Commonwealth gathering. I found (and this opinion was shared by Shri Rajiv Gandhi and Shri H.K.L. Bhagat), that it would not be possible, in 3 months to achieve a high quality production of 250 pages of colour pictures of land and peoples of our country from pre-historic times till today.

I am suggesting that this album be achieved during the next year or so.

Meanwhile, I have suggested to the Prime Minister that the speeches of Jawaharlal Nehru on *India's Foreign Policy* be presented in a deluxe presentation volume for the delegates and others in the forthcoming conference.

The book of the speeches of the first Prime Minister of India have been published by Publications Division in two editions. Both these editions are out of print at the moment.

I am suggesting, therefore, that this important book be brought out in two new editions:

Deluxe edition on good paper and hard bound.

A paperback on modestly good paper.

Both the editions however should carry photographs of Jawaharlal Nehru, the initiator of India's foreign policy with world's statesmen who accepted the Panchsheel, and those with whom he discussed our country's attitudes in regard to peace and co-existence.

I have also suggested that Smt. Indira Gandhi might add a foreword to the new edition of Jawaharlal Nehru's speeches entitled: *India's Foreign Policy* and either T.N. Kaul or G. Parthasarthy or yourself do an afterword, defining the developments of India's foreign policy in the twenty years or so since Jawaharlal Nehru's last speech.

I feel that you might consider editing this volume and see to the implementation of the project.

I have the feeling that this book would be an important part of the dossier you may be planning as from the External Affairs Ministry, because, apart from the fact that there are 40 pages in the Commonwealth Connection in this book, it is the most comprehensive presentation of India's point of view on India and world affairs.

I do hope that you will agree to my plea to become editor of the volume, because only by your active participation in the making of this presentation volume can this book become worthwhile for presentation to delegates of this Commonwealth meet.

With warm regards,

Yours sincerely,

Mulkaj-Knad

(Mulk Raj Anand)

Sh. Kanwar Natwar Singh
Secretary to the Govt. of India
Ministry of External Affairs
New Delhi

25 Cuffe Parade,
Bombay 400005

15 March 1984

My dear Natwar:

I know that living in action as you do, on many planes and aeroplanes, you have no time, in between, to read about the inbetweens of history.

On the other hand, people like me, in the mood of nostalgia, want to remind the new young that we struggled to make myths of new man, in our active lives, as we could not write history.

Actually I don't know how the fragmented mind that I was, myself could have achieved any integrity without putting the 'broken bundle of mirrors' together. And as there were so many pieces to reflect back my memory pictures, I write so many more words than I first intended.

Or perhaps, as my headmaster said: 'Mulk's pen runs away with him.' And yet that past, when we made choices between one way of life to another, has to come through, if only because there was some heroism in a little book dedicated to J.L.N. entitled Apology for Heroism. *The Bubble* is without apologies. I am *unreasonably* sanguine that once you go into it, you will go through, skipping pages of course, but getting to the ethos. After all you may have read Proust.

I claim one week-end from you.

Love for you and the family.

Yours sincerely

Mulk Raj Anand

(Mulk Raj Anand)

31 May 1991

My dear Natwar,

I weep for our adonis—Rajiv!

Of course you, yourself, are likely to be affected in the same way, probably much more because of your active collaboration in promoting our Foreign Policy!

Much as I try to rationalise that no one is indispensable, I still cannot think of anyone who can quite replace the suave, gentle but firm person whom few people understood or wanted to understand!

Inspite of the permutations and combinations in the Congress Party after the election, and whether it comes to power or not (I hope it will), there is bound to be much confusion in the transition from our firm positions of the time when the Congress Party was in power, after two years of misrule and consequent weakening of our position in the world through mistakes in foreign policy.

I do hope that you will be able to renew and extend the whole range of policies and will be in a position to look after that sector of our political life, with others who are still available like Haksar, Tikky Kaul, and Parthasarthy.

One of the immediate things to do might be for you to persuade Damodran, who was helping to produce Krishna Menon's Marathon speech about Kashmir, but which seems to be held up by charlatons of the Krishna Menon Memorial Society for reasons I don't know. In the next few months that answer to Pakistan becomes an important document to circulate to the Governments of the world.

With warm regards

Sincerely

Uncle Mula

25 Cuffe Parade,
Bombay-400005.
Tel: 2181371

24 November 1995

My dear Natwar,

It heartens me to see that while the University of intelligentsia dismisses me as from the older people, as a 'communist', and the younger set as 'not communist enough'—you have dealt with the books qua books, novels albeit, the human condition!

So did Morgan Forster when he said Anand has gone into the streets where I have not been—that is the ethos of the novels shorn of labels.

As for 'isms', I have in *Apology for Heroism*, insisted that the only ism I can broadly accept is *Humanism*.

I must confess that more justice [is] being done in the west. In the Seminar in Johnstown University, Dr. K.D. Verma, contributed a paper: *Understanding Mulk Raj Anand*.

There were several other critiques tracing the anti-Imperialist cause, in the motivations behind the war novels: *Across the Black Waters* and in reaction to Kipling as in the *Conversations in Bloomsbury*. Of course Khushwant Singh has done a three line review of *Conversations* and said: 'Shameless name dropping"!

Some good friends wish to celebrate 12th December[1], I want a low key, tea party, with some good friends. And sing—'Abhi to main jawan hoo', as Hafiz Jalandhari[2] sang!

With warm regards,

Sincerely,

Uncle Mulk

Shri Natwar Singh
D/1/13, Vasant Vihar
New Delhi 110057

---

[1]Mulk Raj Anand's birthday.
[2]Hafeez Jalandhari, an Indo-Pakistani Urdu poet.

25 March 1998

My dear Natwar:

I am writing my reactions to your book: *Profiles & Letters* not as a review, which often gives presumptions judgements by a critic, rather than reaction to books from sympathy an appreciation, depreciation:

It so happens that, after freedom of India from Imperial rule, there have been few politicians or members of Bureaucracy, who have combined in them, fluency in utterance of words on political problems with personal reactions about colleagues with whom they worked.

In earlier years, apart from Mahatma Gandhi, Jawaharlal Nehru and C.F. Andrews, Rajagopalachari, K.M. Munshi, Subash Bose, who wrote books, there were publicists like K.M. Panniker, K.P.S. Menon and Shiva Rao, who wrote of political events, policies and persons. Since freedom, there have been autobiographies by various Presidents of the Republic, active journalism of Frank Morses, R.K. Karanjia, Romesh Thaper, Romilla Thaper, Dom Moraes, Dilip Padgaonker, Ahmed Abbas and women columnists like Shoba De, Tavleen Singh and Nalini Singh. You are, apart from P.N. Haksar and T.N. Kaul, one of the few, or, perhaps, the only executive who has written, from inside the official order, your creative reactions to leaders of Government, writers like E.M. Forster who influenced you deeply, Nirad Chaudhury, who seem to have enjoyed literary quarrels and R.K. Narayan, whose sense of humour in Malgudi stories you see intimate awareness of people by a sensitive writer.

Your position in the I.F.S. brought you into touch with Shri Rajagopalachari, Smt Indira Gandhi, Smt. Vijayalaxmi Pandit, Lord Louis Mountbatten, General Zia-ul-Haq, charming novelist and publicist Han Suyin. And, oddly, enough with Queen of Bollywood Nargis Dutt.

As you decided to write more than laudatory gossip but character sketches, each profile becomes a miniature literary biography,—reflective of the temperaments of the various persons, in the manner of Lytton Strachey whose *Portraits of Five Victorious* set masterly precedent for all later biographers in English literature.

I do not wish to deal with all your reactions, but will take up your profiles of Indira Gandhi, Lord Mountbatten, E.M. Forster, Han Suyin.

In your position as a member of the I.F.S. you found yourself in contact with Smt. Indira Gandhi in April 1966, when you were asked to join the Prime Minister's Secretariat. At that time, P.N. Haksar was Secretary to Prime Minister, while Raja Dinesh Singh was personal Advisor. She put you in charge of organising NAM, the non-aligned meet. Like her father, in whose house she had trained herself to perform the duties of Prime Minister, she had the instinct of choosing those whom she could trust with responsibilities completely. Ofcourse, you were young and had not much experience, but her instinctive awareness of your appreciation with Nehruite policies, and willing devotion, proved her trust in you and you carried out the onerous task of organising both conferences with relatively untrained staff, so that the sessions ran from hour to hour, bringing ideas & policies into focus.

I recall offering to the Prime Minister Indira Gandhi a leaflet about <u>Panchsheel</u> Five Principles. She agreed and I heard that you

(Contd...)

welcomed the simple but *deluxe* brochure which records Prime Minister Nehru's doctrine of solidarity of non-aligned Nations, couched in language of Ashoka's declaration of Dhamma in 3rd century B.C.

After this achievement of yours, Smt. Indira Gandhi asked you to organise the Commonwealth Conference. Again you proved to be a dynamic organiser and Smt. Indira Gandhi began to entrust to you big and small public functions. Then she shared with you readings of books and entrusted you with negotiations such as contacts, on her behalf, with General Zia-ul-Haq, an impossible person in impossible situations of that times which needed suave diplomacy on your part. Altogether, except during emergency, you were able to sustain your official duties in formal-informal manner of a cultured diplomat, with Prime Minister Indira Gandhi.

You know Lord Louis Mountabatten from your student days in 1947, when he visited Scindia's school. But after your contact with him in 1973, in Buckingham Palace reception, when you were Deputy High Commissioner in London, began your personal relations with him. Lord Mountbatten knew your father-in-law, Maharaja Yadavindra Singh, during the time when he was in Delhi to transfer power from British Parliament to India. From your own Princely background, you always seem to have been at ease with aristocracy. But Lord Mountbatten himself grandson of Queen Victoria, remained informal, so that he was at ease with nobility as also with the white, black brown friends, with whom his wife, Lady Edwina Mountbatten, had cordial relations.

The friendship between Jawaharlal Nehru and Lord Mountbatten has become newspaper gossip through the autobiography of Panditji's Secretary, Mathai. He indulged in much vulgar gossip, but those who had the privilege of informal connection with Lord and Lady Mountbatten like you can understand the intimate friendship of the aristocratic couple with Jawaharlal Nehru and Krishna Menon. Lord Mountbatten could dare to confront Bulldog Churchill and put him at ease with a joke, as much as he could relax in a swimming pool with Lady Mountbatten and Jawaharlal Nehru.

As a student in Cambridge, you came into touch with the liberal humanist writer E.M. Forster.

I myself had the privilege of being treated with informal ease by Morgan Forster in the Twenties. And I knew how this humane writer, adopted the motto 'Only connect' as ideal of life.

Unlike some other eminent English writers of that time, J.C. Squira, J.B. Priestley, Hugh Walpole, E.M. Forster was 'Morgan' to old and young. Never patronising. Able to communicate ideas and feelings in conversational asides. From my very first meeting with him when he came to lecture in the Indian Student's union in Gower St. London in 1926, when I asked him whether he had any political intent in his novel: *Passage to India* and he had answered: 'I have only human intent', I could go to him in difficult situations. Infact, it was his generous preface to my novel Untouchable, which was turned down by nineteen publishers, that saved my life, as I had quite seriously considered suicide when my novel was rejected by publisher after publisher. He had the courage to defend D.H. Lawrence's *Lady Chatterley's Lover* against the Home Office ban and the recalcitrance of writers like T.S. Eliot. He spent some days in lobbying with members of Parliament, when I told him that the Punjab Governor, Emerson, had ordered torture of Jayaprakash Narayan in Lahore jail. He was then Chairman of Civil Liberties Union. Ofcourse, you knew him more intimately and longer than any other Indian except R.M. Masood. And, certainly, your indignation against Nirad Chaudhury for saying that: 'E.M. Forster would not be allowed

(Contd...)

to enter his house', showed that such vulgarity of the dissenter Chaudhury, was unworthy of an Indian.

I responded to your profile of Han Suyin from warm feelings of my own for this beautiful and intelligent woman. Unique woman of Chinese–European parentage, she is a doctor by profession, novelist in her spare time, and unacknowledged Ambassador of China. Charming person, who[se] warmth of temperament has won her many friends in East and West. Your informal connection with her, which began in Peking in 1956, when you were appointed to our mission through several years after, you have sustained friendship with her, from which she benefitted as much as yourself. Somehow, Han Suyin, even before her marriage to Indian Engineer Vincent Rathnaswamy, had feelings for India because he had sensed Jawaharlal Nehru's interest in Indian–Chinese friendship even before India became free.

Our enlightened first Prime Minister had foreseen that the political struggle for freedom of India, was parallel to China's emancipatory urges. And, apart from his personal relations with Chang-kai-Sheik and his wife, he had urged, in the UNO, recognition of China by the world body for years.

During the allied struggle against Japanese imperialism, Nehru had connected our own struggle with the Chinese anti-imperialist Movement. Infact, he envisaged that, if India, China and Russia could come together, the East might be able to delimit western power impulses and sustain world peace.

I wonder if Han Suyin had perceived his enlightened projections, in her own vital manner, she seems to have felt that the friendship of India and China would inaugurate culture of peace against the power impulses of the Western States. In her informal private personal connection with Chinese Communists leaders and with Jawaharlal Nehru, she tried to bring about understanding and friendship. If the solidarity broke down this might have been due to derangement of Mao Tse-Tung in his last years.

I feel your profiles are accomplished and sensitive portraits of various personalities, models of literary achievement for young writers of our country. You seem to have learnt from Morgan Forster the meaning of 'Only connect'.

Sincerely

(Mulk Raj Anand)

25 Cuffe Parade,
Bombay 400005.
Tel: 2181371

4 April 1998

My dear friend,

Of course, in the medley of events of the last some months, I have been hoping that the much misunderstood noble lady, Sonia Gandhi might help to bring people to the National Party. And, certainly, her intervention has, despite ugly and ill-mannered names given to her, brought back enough people to the old Party and more may come...

The contradictions of the BJP, and their internal squabbles, may not be very congenial for them. What Atal Bihari Vajpayee is saying reflects his unease...

Anyhow, I am reassured at your return, to Parliament.

I am sure you will improve on Gujral or rather make his goodwill more active.

My review of your book in the informal letter has gone to four papers.

Inspite of my injured leg, which has handicapped my movements, for more than four months, I am in Khandala mostly and able to go on, with self search novel of before the Second World War and I hope I will survive to write up the war period as well.

I am having sent to you a copy of my new novel: NINE MOODS OF BHARATA, just to inspire our brother intellectuals to follow my pilgrimage to Ajanta, Ellora and other monuments. Reprint of my Stories: *Power of Darkness* under title: *Things have*

Way of Working Out is being sent to you by Orient for possible review. Or at least for amusement.

Warm regards,

Uncle Mula

8/2 Ajanta Apartments
74, Colaba Road
Mumbai 400005.

18 June 2003

Dear Natwar,

I am reassured by your note of 29th May that you are well.

These days I am staying in Khandala, to avoid the hectic, polluted life of Bombay.

I continue writing my long autobiographical novel.

I am forced to stay put here as I injured my right leg which is recovering slowly, but which will not encourage me to come to Delhi.

I am reassured to see that you are politically active though I don't see much hope of Congress coming back soon into power. We must persist and your example is there to follow.

With kind regards,

Sincerely

Mala

Shri K. Natwar Singh
1, Akbar Road
New Delhi

VIII

R.K. Narayan
(1906–2001)

'Have you read R.K. Narayan?' asked Forster.

'I have not,' I replied.

'Read him. High-class comedy, without any "isms",' was his advice. It was Spring in Cambridge, the best time of the year.

On returning to India, I read Swami and Friends. I was in splits. It was Narayan's first novel. I was hooked on to him.

In July 1955, the 1953 batch of IFS probationers were on Bharat Darshan. While in Mysore, I left my colleagues to go in search of R.K. Narayan. It was after considerable difficulty that I found him in Yadavgiri. I opened the wicker gate. In the verandah stood a man in shirt and lungi. 'My name is Natwar Singh. I am looking for Mr R.K. Narayan.'

The response was: 'You are talking to him. Are you Khushwant Singh's brother?'

In 1960, Narayan won the Sahitya Akademi Award for his novel, The Guide. In April 1961, he came to Delhi to collect the award. Upon his arrival in Delhi, he contacted me through a mutual friend, Krishna Kripalani, secretary of the Akademi. We had not seen each other for almost six years. I asked if I could do anything for him. 'Two things: Show me the Rose Garden in Rashtrapati Bhawan and take me to Pandit Nehru.'

I achieved both. Nehru was surprised when Narayan told him that he had never seen Delhi before. Narayan presented the prime minister a copy of his latest novel, The Man-eater of Malgudi. Narayan was naturally nervous. Nehru put him at ease, 'Have a look at these albums with photographs of this year's Republic Day parade.' He left for the Parliament asking his daughter to give Narayan and me coffee.

Once, in 1965, Narayan got into serious trouble with his literary agent in New York. His lawyer warned him—if he stayed in New York even for a few hours, he would get a summon to appear in court. I gave him refuge in my apartment and then in the evening saw him off at the Kennedy airport.

Narayan's daughter, Hema, died in 1994. Her death was a devastating blow to him. He took it stoically and with serenity. He dedicated the

American edition of his novel, The Grandmother's Tale and Selected Stories, *to Hema in so many words:*

> *To the memory of my daughter, Hema who selected the additional stories for this volume in order to give it stature: for half a century my companion, friend, philosopher and guide, enriching my life with a granddaughter and a grandson.*

I once took Michael Foot, the British Labour Party leader, to meet RK along with N. Ram. The moment I mentioned that Foot had recently written a biography of H.G. Wells, RK immediately quoted the last lines of Wells's Tono-Bungay *(1909), which he had read sixty years ago: 'We are things that make and pass, out into the sea, upon an unknown mission.'*

R.K. Narayan died in 2001, aged 95.

༄

7 February 1961

My dear Natwar,

Forgive my long silence.

Please don't mind if I continue on the typewriter. I generally alternate between the two, as you know. Nowadays I have got used to the ready-flow of the ball-point, but alas it is not good for more than a line at a time, but the old, fat-in-the-middle aristocratic writing instrument inhibits itself unexpectedly and you can never be sure of the flow. I don't like the typewriter. It makes me sit stiff. So what does it amount to? That one must give up all forms of writing in order to be at peace with one's self.

Well my dear Natji, I am delighted to hear from you. Good of you to write to me twice since Christmas. Since coming back to India, I have been very busy. Don't ask "What were you busy about?" I am not able to give a coherent explanation. I visited Delhi, I wrote on Gandhi for LIFE, I promised articles for magazines and broadcast talks and invariably backed out at the last minute. My mind is buzzing with a new character for a novel and I am writing just five hundred words of it a day and not more, which is again a quarter of my general quota of writing in former days, necessarily so since I am more than twice my own age of about twenty-five years ago when I began writing! What a piece of statistics; I hope it makes some sense. I am also planning on a vast scale the book of mythology for Marshall[1],

---

[1]Marshall Best was vice-president of Viking Press, R.K. Narayan's American publisher.

and I spend some enchanting hours now and then with a real, live pundit who helps me with the research. I am also fixing my house all the time, white-washing, arranging, furnishing and so forth, which leaves me panting at the end of the day. I am just back after two months stay with my grand-daughter. I feel like going back there, now or very soon, abandoning everything. So you have a picture of me. I am delighted to know that you have your apartment now. I shall be delighted to come and stay in your spare-room provided it doesn't bother you in any way. You may rest assured that I will come to you very happily indeed if you have no other guest at the time I arrive. I have no clear plans for coming to New York now as I have been pretty stiff with Harvey[2] when he approached me again, and I won't relax unless he accepts my terms of collaboration. It was Ved Mehta and you that helped me get a new vision of Harvey; thank you both. Please pick up the phone and give my love to Ved. I will write to him sooner or later, but I have been thinking of him a great deal just as I have been thinking of you. I have an invitation to visit Australia in April, after that I may either come to New York (if Harvey proposes it) or visit England for a month. I had an enchanting time in London, and I am tempted to go back there. MAN-EATER was published a couple of days ago by Heinemann and seems to roar its way through if I may judge from the cables I have been receiving.

Please give my love to Santha, and my best wishes for the success of her play. How did Jaffri[3] get into it? How did he get past Faubion? You are only confirming my theory that Jaffri is a

(Contd...)

---

[2]Harvey Breit was producing the celluloid version of R.K. Nayaran's *The Guide*.
[3]Saeed Jaffrey, who acted in the Santha Rama Rau's adaptation of *A Passage to India*.

mimic rather than an actor; of his acting ability he has been the final judge all these days, but the time has come for an objective test, and I will be very interested to know how he comes through. How is Sham sunder? I hope he is flourishing. Please give him my warmest remembrance.

Please keep writing to me as often as you can.

May I exploit you for a small help? I bought a refrigerator from Corvette as you will see from the enclosure. It was in the name of S. Krishnaswami. The refrigerator arrived and is in use. It is a small portable model with legs for which they charged extra. But the legs have not arrived, although, from the bill you will see that I have paid for it. They also said that a booklet explaining its operation would be enclosed with the package. This is not to be found either. Could you take it up with them and ask them to mail both by air-freight? Don't bother about this if you have no time. Forgive the trouble.

Affectionately,

(R.K. Narayan)

If Corvette are willing to supply the legs, please tell them to address the parcel to me straight and not to Krishnaswami.

20 March 1962

My dear Natwar,

I was delighted to have your letter. I am off to Australia today, visiting Adelaide, Melbourne & Sydney. Actually I am writing this in a plane to Delhi, where I shall spend a day with Narayan and Rekha[1]. Of course we will talk about you as much as possible. I am quite charmed to hear that Harvey thought I treated him like a lackey. I don't know who is a lackey, never having had one; but please assure Harvey that I'd never treat a lackey as badly as I would a 'collaborator' that actually turns out to be murderer of a novel. You were handsome to defend me. Actually, do you know that he had approached me again, fourth attempt in four months; he wants to produce it with Zia[2] next season. I have said yes provided I have the final approval of the script. Let us see how it goes this time.

I'm delighted that you are in touch with Marshall. I have not heard from him at all. Our contracts have been satisfactorily concluded. Why should it even be otherwise? I have no idea what went on between my agents and Viking, but always and ever I place implicit trust in my friendship with Marshall, and I would not dream of writing my books for anyone else. You must please convey this to Marshall, as I have been receiving hints now and then of the bothers they face from my agent. I'm spiritually committed to Viking, apart from all other considerations.

(Contd...)

---

[1]Narayan Menon, Director Genreal of All India Radio (AIR), and his wife Rekha.
[2]Zia-moi-uddin, a Pakistani actor residing in London.

I am progressing with my novel, at a somewhat slower pace than I had anticipated. All this amount of travel is partly responsible for it, but I also feel that the book should gain a lot of strength by growing unhurriedly. I am at work on it even in my Australian journeys; we should be able to see a couple of hundred pages before October. I'll tell you how it's getting along. Formerly I used to set 2000 words as my daily quota for a novel, but now I feel that the best results are obtained when I write only 500–1000 words a day. Anyway don't put too much reliance on what I am saying now, as I discover a new theory of writing with each new book each day. There can be no axiom in writing.

Please give my love to Santha & Faubion. I hope you see Natarajan[3] regularly. A thousand thanks for asking me to stay in your flat. I am not quite certain when my next trip to N.Y. is coming off as my Australian visit has come up rather suddenly. Please be writing. I expect to be back in Mysore at the end of April.

Remember me to Sham Sunder.

Affectionately,

(R.K. Narayan)

---

[3]Senior Indian official in the United Nations.

Yadavagiri,
Mysore-2,
S. India

30 August 1962

My dear Natwar:

Why have you not written to me for ages now? I wrote to you about a month ago, did you get the letter? My trip to US is postponed to December. I very much look forward to meeting you at that time in New York. It was awfully good of you to have given my address to Dev Anand who wrote to me and then met me and we have arrived at a very satisfactory arrangement for the production of the GUIDE both in Hindi and English. I am dreadfully busy with a book for Marshal. I hope to complete it by December.

Please give my remembrance to Shayamsunder. Is Shanta in New York or is she out?

Please write to me a long letter about everything.

Affectionately,

(R.K. Narayan)

Mr. K. Natwar Singh,
New York.

29 March 1963

My dear Natwar,

I am delighted to hear from you. I owe you actually three letters. I received the card that you and Santha sent together sometime in December, which came to me last week. I have received your review of Raja Rao's book, which you have done very well indeed. I am very happy to note that Raja Rao is in New York, and if he stays on I shall look forward to seeing him sometime. I am planning to visit New York after I complete my Mythology book, of which a goodly part is already sent for Marshall to read. I am awaiting Marshall's reaction.

Oh, my most understanding friend, you must forgive my saying 'No' to your Forster proposal. I adore him as you do but I can never perform the task of writing a message or an article as you suggest. For one thing, I am unable to take my mind off the book I am desperately trying to finish and secondly I am not good for any such serious, concrete, and responsible job. Please again, forgive me. I give you my sincere good wishes.

Please tell me how Santha is getting along. I owe her an apology and a letter. I received a cable from her long ago about Zia. Since I was at Delhi at that time, I could see the cable only weeks later. In any case, although I agree with her that Zia would have been perfect, I could not have done anything useful as film folk are very un-influencible and generally manage to get along without being clogged by the author's judgement. Please give Santha my love and tell her that I will write to her a long letter if I don't see her before that.

Please ask Raja Rao if he remembers a quarter of a day that we spent together at Madras aeons ago. Tell him that I cherish that memory.

All the best,

Affectionately,

(R.K. Narayan)

Yadavagiri
Mysore-2

10 April 1972

My dear Natwar,

What a joy it was being with you in Delhi. I miss you badly, I tell you. Have you no business which can bring you to Mysore?

I used to be a hopeless letter writer before, but now I promise improvement. I am going to write to you as often as I hear from you, and if I don't hear from you I will always leave one at credit.

I want some more copies of the photo with the P.M., preferably some that include Indira, and the negative of my picture. Could you manage all this? I would hesitate to bother anyone about photographs, but the occasion is special and I feel I can take this liberty with you. Thank you.

Did you manage that piece for The Hindustan Times? How did it go?

I am in a torment about the choice of a theme for my next novel. I am thinking of a new subject each day and rejecting it after a few hours of enthusiastic speculation. The most acceptable seems to be Woman-eater of Malgudi!

Please give my remembrance to Deep[1].

Affectionately,

(R.K. Narayan)

---

[1] An intimate friend of mine. She was one of the most beautiful women of her generation.

Mysore.

25 October 1978

My dear Natwar,

I am delighted to hear from you after all these months of silence. But I was in touch with Sharada Prasad[1] and he kept me informed of your welfare. When you are in this country next, please let me know so that we may meet. I note that Hem and children are now here. When I go to Delhi next, I will try to telephone to her.

Many thanks for accepting Anthony Curtis's[2] assignment. I shall look forward to your piece. Don't spare me. It is very pleasant for me to see my earlier works reprinted by Heinemann methodically within two or three years. My handicap all along has been my agency in London, which handled my manuscripts since 1937 but functioned like a government office in a routine manner without any push or initiative. Graham Greene pleaded with me to change my agents, which I have done now, and I hope my British contacts will improve with all new work, although the earlier books are still with the old agency.

What am I writing now? Good question, but I am unable to answer it coherently. I suspect I have lost the patience to write a novel, which may tie me up for months and months. My inclination is all to write short stories, long and short ones: the possibility of variety in themes and economy in the writing appeals to my mind, and I am plodding on in the afternoons writing a few

(Contd...)

---

[1] Information adviser to Indira Gandhi at the time.
[2] Editor of the *Financial Times*, London.

hundred words as I have always done, but God alone can have a knowledge of what it will all turn out to be! I am reading plenty of worthless American novels, in quantity and contents all alike! America has ruined the world of letters through its commercial expertise and best-seller 'syndrome', and computerized formula fiction with its million sales.

I read your article on Rajaji with great pleasure. Very readable and interesting indeed. SWARAJYA is struggling to revive—but lacks capital, writers, editorial aim, and competence. When these handicaps are overcome it may find enough readers to support it. I find it very amateurish and A.S.R.'s[3] own feature affected and inane. This is my private opinion, please keep it to yourself as I would not like to upset A.S.R. or Sadasivam[4], who are my good friends.

Do you recognize this typewriter on which I am composing this letter? It is the Olympia, which you sold me in New York for 60 dollars nearly fifteen years ago.

Where is Bhagwat[5]? Please give him my warmest remembrance when you write to him next. I greatly look forward to seeing him when I am in U.S. next spring. I have an invitation to visit Berkeley for one month as a 'Regent' lecturer. It is some chair, I think; and I am looking forward to it.

Please keep in touch,

Affectionately,

(R.K. Narayan)

---

[3]A.S. Raman, then Editor of *The Illustrated Weekly of India*.
[4]Husband of classical singer M.S. Subbulakshmi.
[5]Bhagwat Singh, my elder brother.

15 Vivekananda Road,
Yadavagiri
Mysore-570002.

My dear Natwar,

Your piece on the 'Tiger of Malgudi' is marvelous—so full of understanding and packed with memories of our association—since that memorable day of your visit 'with' me in 1955. I never realized that nearly three decades have elapsed since that auspicious moment.

I am happy that you appreciate Raja as a being. After writing this novel I have lost sight of distinction between human beings and animal beings! I do not know if it is good or bad as a philosophy.

Your style is sharp and precise and your review is not only a review but a lovely vignette—God bless you—with a hundred years too. When you can spare a few minutes please do write to me.

I have reserved a copy of my novel, the American edition which has a picturesque jacket, for the P.M, to be presented to her in person, but so far I have not found an excuse to visit Delhi. So ultimately, I shall mail it, I suppose.

I have signed with Viking for a new novel, which is not shaping up convincingly yet—though obsessing my mind.

Please convey my warmest remembrances to Hem and the children.

Affectionately

(R.K. Narayan)

Soundarya Apartments
164 A-1, Eldams Road, Alwarpet,
Madras-600018

1 May 1995

Mr. K Natwar Singh
D-l/37 Vasant Vihar
New Delhi-110057.

My dear Natwar,

I was thinking of you a great deal the last few days and I was delighted to have your phone call this afternoon though it was all-too brief, since I wanted to say so much to you. I tried to call you back without success. Perhaps your number is changed. Do write to me about yourself and Sharada Prasad, two friends, who are most valuable in my life.

What are your writing now? I read your column in *Frontline* with great pleasure. Ram[1] meets me almost every evening after dinner and stays for an hour or two discussing various matters. Tell me about your son and daughter and give my warm remembrance to Hem.

Yours affectionately,

(R.K. Narayan)

---

[1] N. Ram, former editor-in-Chief of *The Hindu*.

Yadavagiri,
Mysore-2.

Dear Natwar

You, bad boy, never told me what you were up to—and now this morning's *Hindu* springs a surprise on me by publishing a review of your Jawaharlal! A good review, and God bless you with success, both in literature and foreign service; but I find it hard to forgive your demure silence. (I have had to change my pen at this spot as the one I started with has begun to behave like a stencilling stylus withholding the ink under all circumstances— Parker 61, the executive pen, the expense account pen, fit for a gift but alas not for writing).

I met Santha a week ago in Bombay, and I spent a lovely morning talking to her. It did me good to find her in her old form.

Please remember me to G.P.[1], and give him my best wishes. I hope his wife has recovered her health now. I met him [in] London last year, when he was passing an anxious time over his wife's health.

I met Mr Natarajan[2] at Madras a month ago. I was greatly distressed to note that their family in finding life in the Mother country not quite agreeable; and all his children are agitating to be taken back to New York!

I am at work on my novel, but plan to write the last few chapters in New York, where I hope to come at the end of October. Where will you be? May I hope to have the joy of meeting you as often as your other occupations and preoccupations will permit?

(Contd...)

---

[1] G. Parthasarathi, Indian ambassador to the United Nations.
[2] An Indian official working at the United Nations Secretariat.

You will be happy to know that Harvey Brait's[1] case was quashed in me arbitration. He can never bother me again.

Affectionately,

(R.K. Narayan)

---

[1] A literary agent.

IX

Krishna Hutheesing
(1907–1967)

❧

Krishna Nehru was Motilal Nehru's youngest child. She was charming, amusing and a fairly competent writer but lacked the charisma of her brother and sister. Her autobiography, With No Regrets *(1945), which she wrote at the age of 37 was widely read. Her brother read it in Ahmednagar jail and praised in an affectionate way.*

She admitted her sons, Harsha and Ajit, in Scindia School, Gwalior, in July 1944. Soon she took to me and I recall her endearing ways, to this day. In 1965, Krishna Masi—(Masi as in 'Aunt'), as I had come to call her by then—stayed with me in New York. By then I had got to know several publishers. She was then working on a biography of her niece, Indira, for which she was in search of an American publisher. In that context, I introduced her to a Director at MacMillan. The book, Dear to Behold: An Intimate Portrait of Indira Gandhi, *was published in 1969, two years after Masi's death. She passed away in London in November 1967. A couple of days later, I accompanied Indira Gandhi to Krishna Masi's cremation in Bombay.*

∾

30 March 1958

My dear Natwar,

I thank you for your letter of the 22 March and also the one you wrote on hearing of Maulana's death. I was in Delhi for nearly a month where I went to recoup and I rested a great deal and came back feeling much better. I was there during the exciting days of TTK's[1] resignation and I attended Parliament regularly throughout the three days of debate.

I met the R.K. Nehrus[2] at a lunch Bhai gave for Ho-Chi-Minh[3], to which they invited themselves by repeatedly saying that they were leaving for their son's wedding and might not get a chance of seeing Bhai, so at the last moment he invited them! Mrs R.K. tried to show off her Chinese, and when I mentioned to her that you spoke rather well she shrugged her shoulders and said that it wasn't correct Chinese that you spoke and that you had to take a lot of lessons in Peking. Anyhow her Chinese did not seem to go down with Ho-Chi-Minh and his party. So, just to be difficult I started talking to them in French which I knew she did not understand. This upset her quite a lot. I do not think either of them are happy to go to Cairo.

I shall be in Bombay round about the 10th of May and so you can certainly come and stay with us. I do not know why you

(Contd...)

---

[1]T.T. Krishnamachari, Nehru's Finance Minister.
[2]Second cousin of Nehru; Secretary General, Ministry of External Affairs and Ambassador to China and Egypt.
[3]President of Vietnam, 1954–69.

are under the impression that Harsha and Ajit will be here then. Ajit has to do three months' work in some factory in Germany as part of his Course, and Harsha is going to do six weeks or more of work in some newspaper office in Minneapolis. He is not willing to stay on in America. So, after that he may return to England and continue doing his Law. Harsha has been begging me for several months to go to him and hence I want to do so. I have not quite planned when to leave, but it might either be at the end of May or the beginning of June. In case I am not able to get a passage then, I might go a little earlier. But, I should be here around the 10th when you are expected to arrive.

I wonder if you could do me a favour. A friend of mine, who returned recently from Hong Kong, bought a short coat there, which had black Chinese silk or satin on one side and white fur, something like Astrakhan, on the inside. Actually it was reversible. You could wear it both ways, with the white fur outside and the black silk lining inside or the other way round. It was very smart and light, and not too expensive. I am giving you below the address of a friend of mine in Hong Kong—she is a Chinese married to a Parsi—to whom I am also writing and I will tell her to try and get this and give it to you. But in case she cannot or if you can find something like it in Peking and bring it to me, I shall be very grateful. The coat length was about 29" long, may be 27" or less. But it was very light and as I have said very smart looking, yet very warm and it would help a lot to carry a thing like that instead of a thing which is heavy and hefty.

Yes. I have seen Tara's book and read bits and pieces of it only, because she gave a copy to Bhai and being an American publication it is not sold here. I see now that it is going to be

---

[3]C.R. Mandy, editor, *The Illustrated Weekly of India.*

serialised in the *Illustrated Weekly*. I did not see Mandy's[3] review, but I was told that it was a very flattering one. The little I read, I couldn't make out as to what the story was about or what exactly it meant to depict.

More when we meet and do try and find out about the coat. I shall look forward to having a long chat with you here.

With love,

m⟨d⟩r

(Krishna Hutheesing)

P.S. My friend's address is:
Mrs. Anne Ruttongi,
2 Conduit Road, Hong Kong. Or
The Office address is:
C/o Ruttonji & Co.,
Shell House,
Hong Kong.

PS: Raja says, if possible, could you bring some Chi Pai Shih scrolls. We would pay you in rupees here—For the coat, if Anne gets it & you have money pay her—If not, I'll arrange.

Djakarta

13 April 1959

Natwar—

I wrote the post card last evening. We are in a modern flat but not one servant speaks English so we are completely cut off from the world—cannot even phone. I'm fed up to the hilt. Appointments are made and we rush off only to find the young man from the foreign office who takes us around got the timings wrong!! The word 'efficient' does not exist in the Indonesian dictionary. We have been asking for the daily newspapers but have not received any for a week! Last night we dined with Mr Khosla and he gave us a whole lot of Indian papers which Raja and I devoured. Could you do me a favour? I wrote to the Hindustan Times from Bombay and had spoken to Sri[1] in Delhi, to send me the H.T. by airmail regularly. They did not do so. Could you pay the subscription for it by *air mail* from May 1st for a year or 6 months and let me know what it is? I shall send a cheque but please see that it is sent.

If you are ever posted here, don't accept—quit the External Affairs but don't come here. We met young Haksar who is 3rd secretary here—seems nice. Do you know him?

Af.fly,

mgr

---

[1]Sri Mulgaonkar, Editor of *Hindustan Times*, New Delhi.

PS: No one—repeat no one—(not the foreign office—not hotels—not even our Embassy and not even the post office knows the rates of postage—a letter or a P.C. cost the same; hence my extravagance.

K. H.

21 April 1959

We met Suyin but only once. Naturally we spoke of you for a while but I did not get another chance. We are on our way to Bangkok then Angkor Vat back to B'kok & home on the 29th.

With love

mädi

(Krishna Hutheesing)

Natwar dear,

So M.O.[1] has won?! What now? What hope for any honest person in the land that is our Bharat?

We returned on the 29th to find Tsing-Ju's[2] eye looking very bad. Took it to hospital & was told she was blind! They had been treating her since I brought her last September; and said it was 'nothing serious'. Have been very upset—unable to do any work. Took Tsing-Ju to the eye-specialist who confirmed her blindness—such is life!

I want to send a small parcel to Berit, Ajit's ex-girlfriend, to Oslo as she wrote & invited me to her wedding.

Love,

mași

(Krishna Hutheesing)

---

[1]M.O. Mathai, Nehru's private secretary.
[2]Masi's pet dog.

28 June 1959

Dear Natwar,

Once again I write to introduce you to a young American lad, Kevin Cahill (pronounced केविन केहिल) who is studying medicine & came to us with a letter of introduction from one of our very dear friends, Dr Edgar Mayar. I shall be grateful for anything you can do for him.

I am enclosing a letter from K. Ram—Bhai's secretary to whom I'm writing separately also. Will you arrange for Kevin to meet Ram—Kevin wants his copy of Bhai's 'Discovery' autographed—that's all.

Will write at length later. The monsoon has broken at last & so it is slightly cooler.

With love

mcdr

(Krishna Hutheesing)

25 July 1959

Natwar dear,

Your letter which came this evening was most welcome—though the news made me mad—I must not get excited! Five days ago we had Roger Baldwin to dinner & 5 others—a small party. I was quite well all day & night up till dinner was announced. As I walked in, I got a twinge of pain but I curbed it throughout dinner though it kept increasing. As soon as dinner was over, which I had not been able to eat, I staggered into my room in agony. A friend of mine Makia (Lady) Bhiwandiwalla came behind me & called Raja. I was doubled up in pain, as I've had off & on for years but this was the worst I've known. R. rang for our doctor who was out—his assistant advised Coramine drops in brandy which R. gave me and I vomited & passed out completely. I felt very ashamed of myself next day but R. says I came to and again passed out—I slept after 3 p.m. having had the attack at 10 p.m. sharp. I've been in bed since strictly supervised by a dragon of a friend who would not leave me one moment. To-day my cardiogram was taken here & though Dr Vakil said he did not think it was 'heart', I had had certain symptoms e.g. profuse sweating, etc. so I have to go slow—not get out of bed till the 29th and then not go out for a week.

26th—some people came & I could not finish—am feeling much better today but am glad of the doctor's orders... I do not feel like going out. I hardly see Raja—he is so busy with the S. Party[1] which gives him little swatantrata[2]. I am keeping aloof

(Contd...)

---

[1]The Swatantra Party (1959–74) was an Indian liberal-conservative political party founded by C. Rajagopalachari.
[2]Freedom

because I do not like Masani[3] & Co but I do admire Rajaji—he arrives this evening. So Raja will be busier. I am glad, only when I've been so ill I've had to remain all alone from 9 am till 8 or 9 pm! Not very pleasant when one is ill. However—this is life—news of the boys is good but I wish they were here. Mrs P[4] told Harsha there was no room for him so I wrote to Sir so & so, Lord so & so, etc & asked them to find him digs—that did it! He is at 9 KPG but won't stay—more later.

Love,

Mesr

(Krishna Hutheesing)

---

[3]Minoo Masani, Member of Parliament.
[4]Her sister, Vijaya Lakshmi Pandit.

2 April 1960

Natwar dear,

Heard the glad tidings that you have been 'promoted'! Congratulations. It's a pity you will come after I've returned home. Anyhow, Harsha will be here or in Cambridge.

Saw Forster's play—wasn't too good but seem to be going down well with the English public. My sister says the fact that an Englishwoman was raped in a beautiful cave is what excites the imagination of all the frustrated people here!

Love,

mdr

(Krishna Hutheesing)

P.S. You should get married before you come on this assignment— so the elders think!!

Look forward to seeing you.

Who is coming here—it's an astounding set up—no office— shopping-parties—hair dressers—more parties—cancellations of programmes due to ill health but no social cancellations!

Natwar—your letter—my sister has played yet another foul trick on me and stabbed me behind my back.[1] I am coming to Delhi on the 13th evening by plane—10.30 on something, with Raja, and I am going to have it out for once and all with the P.M. I shall return on the 17th if not earlier. Tell Sri.

Love,

Masi

(Krishna Hutheesing)

---

[1]Masi refers here to one of their usual quarrels.

22 July 1961

My dear Natwar,

I received your letter this morning—the first one written by you either to me or to Harsha since we left Delhi. I have no idea what Harsha's impression was, but mine was certainly this, that you are following in the footsteps of all the others in the Ministry of External Affairs by behaving in a way that is vague and undetached.

Congratulations on being posted to the U.N. Permanent Mission and also for having got rid of your appendix. Ajit and Amrita's address is:

Apartment 4F, 17 West, 67th Street; New York 23 and is in the telephone directory. Harsha's address in London is:

72, Pembrook Road; London W. 8.

He is sharing a flat with two friends of his who are up at Kings with him (Tel. Western 8752)

Will you please let me know as soon as it is possible: 1. Whether you are going via. Bombay. 2. Whether you can take a small parcel containing three or four blouses for Amrita and a few odd presents like cuff-links etc. for some people, who I owe a present to in New York. 3. If you are not going via Bombay could I send this parcel to you to Delhi. Raja has been going off and on to Calcutta and has been away this time nearly a fortnight. Ever since Harsha has gone, I have been very lonesome and depressed—mostly on account of Harsha and his inability to find his feet in India. I have been trying to work hard and have finished one book, which has gone to the publishers and am carrying with the next one, but have in-between had bouts of high fever and all sorts of other troubles, which I presume are due to old age.

With love,

Krish

(Krishna Hutheesing)

Ajit's home number is:-
    Susquehanna 7-8796.
    Office, I think, Whitehall 3-Ex 676, but I'm not sure. You will find it under Carl M Locb Rhoades. Wall St.

23 December 1964

Dear Natwar,

This is a brief & hurried letter to thank you for your Xmas card & to tell you that I am leaving for the States on the 2nd Jan., reaching on the 4th by Air India flight 103 around 14.55 p.m. I am on a lecture tour and will be met by my friend Mrs Harry (Edith) Lapirow of 99, Main St, Kennebunk, Maine as she knows the schedule which starts from Maine. I will be with her at the Plaza, New York & leave on the 6th with her for Kennebunk. The rest I do not know. But c/o Edith will always find me.

Though I have been very remiss in writing, I have not forgotten you or any of my friends. Raja & I have had a hellish two years & after my brother died, apart from feeling the world had come to an end, worse calamities befell us. We are quite shattered & this is why Raja, Indira, my American sponsors & friends there & here forced me to take this trip. I hate leaving Raja but I know I'll crack up if I do not. Once there, away from familiar surroundings, I hope it will help & also I might be able to get Raja over.

I look forward very much to meeting you, somewhere. Please keep in touch & forgive me for not having written. You will I am sure understand when I tell you all that has happened.

Yours, with love

mzdr

(Krishna Hutheesing)

(Contd...)

P.S.: I've written twice to Sunil[1] and to Bijju asking them to have me met at the airport to facilitate customs, etc. I've lost a lot of weight & feel ill & miserable & dread the ordeal of waiting hours in customs sheds. If you can come it will be wonderful—

mdr

---

[1]Sunil Roy, Consul General in New York.

Cincinnati 37, Ohio.

21 January 1965

Natwar dear—

Jimmy *did not* phone me, nor Sunil. If you speak to Bijju again, tell him to kindly *leave a note* at the Plaza or tell you:

1) Whether or not I can meet Indu at the airport on the 25th only if a host of others are not going to be present. *If* they *are*, I'll go to the Carlyle & await her there.

2) I hope you meet us & could you bring my suitcase in your car as I want to take out things I do not want & re-pack properly.

3) I want to buy a suitcase—Edith has so far been paying all my expenses & I can't go on letting her do so for every little & big thing.

4) If Bijju can possible give you some idea of Indu's programme in New York it would help. If not I'll accept other invitations & may have to refuse anything they & Indu have together to which they *might* (?) invite me but I doubt they will. I'm going out to dinner on the 24th night with some old friends—On the 27th after the exhibition, I'd like to give dinner to Edith, Linda & her husband & you. Do you have any cooking arrangements in your flat & ingredients, etc.? If so, I could cook a meal there & it would be more cozy, and of course cheaper!

5) Could you spare a couple of bottles of Scotch & one Gin & one Vermouth for us at the Plaza?

(Contd...)

217

Forgive my troubling you, Natwar, I don't know who else to ask and no one seems to worry about me in our Embassy or Consulate.

With love,

mar

(Krishna Hutheesing)

X

Han Suyin

(1917–2012)

I arrived in Peking as Third Secretary in the Embassy in July 1956. I was staying at the unglamorous Hsin-Chio hotel. On my very first morning, when I went up to the dining room for breakfast, I failed at ordering for any as the menu was written in Chinese and the comrade waiters spoke no English. Just as I was beginning to despair, in walked a lady. She looked stunning. Furtively, I kept looking at her. Where had I seen her? Could she be her. Of course not. What would she be doing in China? But she looked so familiar. I scribbled a note on the back of the menu and asked one of the comrade waiters to take it up to the lady. 'I am starving and can't order my breakfast. Are you Han Suyin? If so, can you please help?' Her answer toppled the linguistic barrier. 'Yes, I am Han Suyin. Come and join me.'

Thus began a friendship that lasted five decades. In 1980, in her autobiography, My House Has Two Doors, *she wrote, '...Natwar Singh, a young Embassy secretary, a delightful companion for rambles and a devotee of the English writer E.M. Forster...is learning Chinese, but appeared in no hurry to become an expert.'*

I left Peking for India on 2 May 1958. On my way back, I stopped in Hong Kong to meet Han Suyin. We took a tram ride to go up to Victoria Peak. The view of the Hong Kong harbour was breathtaking. I uttered an unoriginal remark: 'Here be the peace that passeth all understanding.' Suyin added: 'Peace that passeth all misunderstanding.'

In the decades that followed, we met in different parts of the globe. The last time was in Lausanne, Switzerland, in 2004. Dementia had set in. It was heartbreaking to see her so helpless. She died in 2012, at the age of 85.

I keep reading her immortal novel, A Many-Splendoured Thing *(1952), an autobiographical novel covering her passionate love affair with an English correspondent who died covering the Korean War in 1950. The film* (Love Is a Many-Splendored Thing, 1955) *with William Holden and Jennifer Jones was, however, far too gooey for my taste.*

39, Upper Pickering Street,
Singapore

23 July 1958

Dearest Natwar,

Thank you very much for your letter of July 9th. I notice that you are in the exalted post of Under Secretary, Ministry of External Affairs, which is more important than Chief Secretary or Minister because it is Under Secretaries who make up the bosses' minds. I shall probably have to come to you for an Indian passport one of these days and I hope that after due investigation, you will give it to me. I promise to go on thinking well of Indians. After all, they seem quite indispensable in this extraordinary world of today. Whenever there's trouble anywhere, it's poor Mr. N. (not N for Natwar) who gets long letters from everybody just as if he was everybody's kind uncle. What a good time you must have comparing all the letters you get from the various statesmen; which was the longer, Khrushchev's or Eisenhower's?

Thank you for your comments on my book[1], I am sorry that there is some self pity in earlier chapters but, dear Natwar, I think it is because you are not a woman used as a mattress that you notice it. Of all the hundreds of women that I have known who have complained of scenes similar to those you find on pages 21 and 22, the most predominant characterization was self-pity. In another ten or fifteen years when you get to be my age, perhaps you will not think it self-pity. I can understand that you don't like John but I think the reason is that you have got some hero-worship of the stiff upper lip in your upbringing but I, as a doctor, see them when their upper lip is not only unstiffened, but positively drippy.

(Contd...)

---

[1]She refers to her novel *The Mountain Is Young.*

Finally, as to Unni, when did you ever know a man worthy of the love he was given? It is not one's worth that merits another's love but it is due to circumstances. Of course Unni is just an ordinary man and quite unworthy of Rukmini's sacrifice but he happens to be the incarnation of the principle of sex and that is the theme of the book and if you will notice, he keeps on saying that he is only a man and he is forever being given love and honour beyond his due. Again perhaps, in another ten years, you will understand when the same thing happens to you as indeed it may.

I am going to Europe in September with Yungmei as my secretary and we shall certainly pass through Delhi. I shall send you a cable a week or ten days in advance. Can you reserve us rooms in a good hotel? I do not think I will stay with Malcolm[2] this time, much as I like him. The gap between East and West to my mind is getting wider, I mean the gap in emotions and understanding and I view this with great concern. Only in your country do I find an attempt to understand both sides and bring them together but at the same time, I am alarmed by the price you have to pay for it. Perhaps we can have a long talk in Delhi.

I am sending enclosed a letter for Tikki[3]. He wrote to me but I have inadvertently misplaced his letter but I am sure you know where he is. I am also enclosing a picture which I thought you might like.

Affectionately,*

Elizabeth

P.S. I have just found Tikki's letter so I am writing direct.

---

*Elizabeth was one of Han Suyin's names.
[2]Malcolm MacDonald, Commissioner General of the UK in Singapore, and later High Commissioner of the UK in India.
[3]A close friend of Han Suyin, T.N. Kaul later became foreign secretary in the Ministry of External Affairs.

39, Upper Pickering Street,
Singapore

30 August 1958

Dear Natwar,

Thank you very much for the review which I liked. Thank you for being kind, although I think that you are one of the people who would like to cut Shakespeare by half and reduce *Wuthering Heights* to stripe in a bubble-speaking comic for easier mental digestion. I think you have done your best but had you waited another ten years, you would have understood the book[1] much better. So many people do not understand it, men I mean. Women understand it because they know what they really feel and either they love it, or are revolted, depending on whether they are frustrated or not.

As I probably told you in my last letter, I shall be coming to Delhi on my way home as I am to be Guest of Honour at Foyle's Literary Luncheon in London on October 10th and before that, I have to fit Yungmei into an educational institution for a year.

All other news when we meet.

Yours ever,

(Han Suyin)

P.S. Elizabeth has just dashed out on a case and says, "Sign the letters, Lynn".

---

[1]She refers to her book, *The Mountain Is Young.*

SAVOY HOTEL LONDON

TELEPHONE, TEMPLE BAR 4343   TELEGRAMS, SAVOTEL LONDON

3 October 1958

K. Natwar-Singh Esq., I.C.S.,
22 Delhi Gymkhana Club,
New Delhi 1, India.

Dear Natwar,

I am writing from London, where I have just arrived. I have had your letter, and this is to say that I shall be arriving in Delhi around the 24th October if all goes well. I don't want to stay with Malcolm, I would love to stay with you, but I can't be your mother or your sister or your wife, and as for your daughter—ha ha! Besides, I think Vincent will be coming up to Delhi, and so please will you book me a room in a hotel for two or three days?

Apart from that, please come to fetch me at the Airport because I can't stand the Customs any more. They seem to be worse in your country than in any other, and last time I was in Calcutta they were saying things like: 'Why do you come to India so often?' They should be terribly happy that a lot of nice tourists like myself, who don't bring their toilet paper and their drinking water with them, do come to India. But perhaps they will find out in a few years.

Anyway, I'm not blaming you or the External Ministry for that.

I would hate to be interviewed on the All India Radio Network, it's much too English. But apart from all that, of course I would love to see you and I hope I will see lots of you in New Delhi.

Yungmei is fine, and as she has only just arrived and is a cautious person she will not tell me what she thinks of Old Blighty. If I had time I would go down to Cambridge to see your friend E.M. Forster, and I hope by now Cape has traced Brian Abel-Smith. Yes, I did run into Sharma[1] in Geneva, but not his Russian wife. However, I am carrying a terrible camera, which keeps on snapping open so that I have to put it in my suitcase instead of hanging it tourist-wise round my neck, for his wife; and also an alarm watch. Yes, it is a watch with an alarm, and the alarm goes off suddenly and it frightens me so much that I can't wear it either. But Sharma was absolutely delighted with those two objects, and I shall leave them with you in New Delhi for his Russian wife.

I enclose a Foyle's blurb, just because I am sure you know far more people than I do, and I would love to listen to your reminiscences when I get to Delhi.

Love,

Suyin

(Han Suyin)

---

[1]P.N. Sharma, well-known Indian photographer, known to Nehru.

39, Upper Pickering Street
Singapore

1 January 1959

Mr. Natwar Singh,
22, Gymkhana Club,
NEW DELHI.

Dear Natwar,

Many good wishes for 1959. Are you marrying your Nepalese princess? If you are, don't forget to invite me to the wedding. I am looking forward to all those elephants which you say you will have in your wedding procession.

I cut out these little news items on your country and am sending them to you as I hope you will clear up the mystery for me. The item says that the U.S. Agricultural Dept. in Washington reports that there will be a record breaking rice crop in India. I thought Delhi was the capital of India and not Washington! Is this a sign of things to come? Has India really been bought up lock, stock and barrel by American dollars so that news of crop harvests can only be sent from Washington, D.C.?

Lately I have received any number of news items all quoting Indian sources and all highly critical of China. I hope there will be some people in your country even-minded enough to see it would be a disaster for Asia should India be maneuvered into becoming the Voice of America.

Affectionately, as always

Suyin

(Han Suyin)

2 Cuttings enclosed.

Dear Natwar,

Your friend Dom Moraes (friend to the Narayans) has I saw in the local newspaper abjured India, insulted Nehru, and asked for a British passport. You may remember the half hour we all spent together with his father, and the terrible argument which I had with his father. When I say terrible, I mean that I enjoyed it, of course.

I could not stomach some of the silly things Dom wrote, particularly as our local newspaper, which hates anything Asian (it is in English, and run by the usual type of people), not only gave his article a half page, but ran a huge picture of Dom's profile, so that he took up ONE WHOLE PAGE in the *Straits Times*. I don't know what they did to lionize him in England in certain circles. I suppose now he will write a book called: "Gone Away Forever from the Land of Tyranny and Nehru."

Anyway I am asking Mrs. Russell-King[1] to send you a copy of my open letter to him, which was also published, but with much less fanfare.

Astonishingly, your Indian representative here, in Singapore, is apologizing to everybody over Goa. He is not fit to be an Indian, I think. His wife comes from Bombay, is half Portuguese, and plays golf with all the highbrows. Perhaps that is why!

I am sorry I forgot to sign my letter to you. My Christmas cards are ALWAYS mailed by Mrs. King, and it is clever of you to recognize her handwriting instead of mine. I was away this year and asked her to sign them for me. I do not, like you, however, feel that this is loathsome. Next year you will get no card at all.

---

[1] Her friend and agent.

I am signing this, as usual, but I am very tempted NOT to sign it. After all, what's in a name, especially when one types it, as YOU do.

Affectionately,

Suyin

(Han Suyin)

P.S. I am suing your friend Shirle Gordon for some money which she owes me.

Address: Permanent Mission of India to U.N.
3 East 64th St. New York 21.

37 Montoie
Lausanne.

14 April 1977

My dear Natwar and Hem,

We shall be away in Yougoslavia from the 10th evening of May, until about the 17th or 18th. I suggest that you come on the ninth; we can reserve you a charming little hotel, only 70 swiss francs for a double bedroom for a night. In this way, I can show Hem all the flat and how to work things etc., not that she does not know, but that it will make things easier for her. Then on the 10th evening or afternoon we go to Zurich and we shall catch the plane to Ljubljana. We hope you will be our guests all through, and I hope this schedule will be acceptable to you.

I am very happy to have you here; I only hope that, in another occasion to come, you will be my guests at our mountain resort, which is tiny, but very very beautiful.

Khushwant Singh is very desultory; he has not sent me any copies of ILLUSTRATED WEEKLY with my articles, although this is customary for an author. I also have with him round 46 photographs of all kinds, and now I am a bit worried because it took a lot of time and trouble to get the photographs in China, and I do hope nothing happens to them between his printing them and my receiving them.

I am now writing PHOENIX HARVEST, which is the book about my life from 1949 to 1976. Had Chiang Ching (Madame Mao) come to power, I would have been in a terrible position because I would have had to denounce her. Only Asians, like yourself, realize how we operate on several planes; I did not like her, she did not like me. But this was not important. What was important was that from 1975 onwards I felt she could not be a leader of China, because she did things in such a terrible arbitrary way.

I do hope that the friendship between India and China will go on prospering; after all, we have such clearly delimited zones of influence, and China is not interested in extending beyond it; Japan, Korea, and Vietnam and maybe the Philippines are China's "zone". India has had a wonderful and fantastic zone of cultural influence in the past, and this is far more enduring than any other. I think that westerners do not understand how enduring and profound cultural influence is.

Please let me know quickly whether you can come to Lausanne on May 9. There is a good bus from Geneva to Lausanne, directly from airport to railway station. We shall meet you here at the Lausanne railway station and bring you to the hotel which is very near for one night. Then the next day the whole flat is yours.

With much love from both of us to both of you,

Suyin

(Han Suyin)

37 Montoie,
Lausanne
Switzerland.

14 July 1978

My dear Natwar

Thank you for your letter. No, I never received the two letters you mention, only the last postcard, to which I replied, from Lusaka.

Glad to hear that you are in great shape, and looking forward to your ancestors! I think ancestors are good value anywhere; and yours should be. In fact, it is probably because of your ancestors that you keep sane in this mad mad world. And Hem too. I also have solid ancestors behind me; which is why I also am relatively sane (I hope).

I am very tempted to come to Lusaka, and you may see us descend upon you in early 1979!

I am at the moment engaged in trying to see Sihanouk[1]. That is because I cannot stomach anymore the kind of treatment he is getting. I have told the Chinese that the Cambodians are being very silly (that is a weak word for my strong emotions on the subject). And that if they want any good, Sihanouk must come back...I don't think the Chinese are against it by any means, but they are always over-cautious about giving advice to friends (they sometimes give too much lecturing to enemies). Anyway, HAN SUYIN IS ANGRY!!! I have asked to see Sihanouk. I don't think I will succeed, but I must try.

Going to China in August, will be back in October (end of).

---

[1] Prince Norodom Sihanouk, King of Cambodia.

Much love to you and to Hem, and glad the children are adapting well. How is Tikki? Won't it be nice to see all old friends in New Delhi? I intend to stay with you, as a sort of parasite (Chinese fungus) for at least a week!!!

Vincent is coping well with the son problem. It's not over by any means, but we are coping.

With love to you and Hem,

Suyin

(Han Suyin)

6 August 1979

My dear Natwar,

I think a lot of you these days, afflicted with the commonwealth conference, having to put up with E II[1] and all that sort of thing. I do so wish that I could have made myself clear this year to come to visit you; but it is quite possible that now you may be whisked away to Delhi in the new setup that looms in India. Anyway, this is just to say that my love and affection for you and Hem remain entire, even if it is not so demonstrative as it ought to be.

I have been reading again your book on EM Forster and once again to thank you for dedicating it to me. You loom in my book which will be published next year in English, this year in French: MY HOUSE HAS TWO DOORS and which is China and me (in that order, please!) from 1949 to 1979. Of course you, your clear minded vision of things between China and India, did an enormous lot to teach me how to live and how to think. Bless you and I shall never forget it.

Much love,

Suyin

(Han Suyin)

---

[1] Queen Elizabeth II

31 March 1984

My very dear Natwar and Hem,

Back from two and a half months in China, I read in the Indian paper about the PADMA BUSHAN being bestowed on you, Natwar, for your services, and though my letter is surely belated, yet I want to write and tell you how happy I am that your great services, the dedication, effort, work and TACT and SKILL which you put into everything you do, are at last recognized.

It must be a very busy time for you; we read of troubles in India, violence especially; but I do hope it will all quieten down as much of it seems quite pointless and absurd.

My projects for this year are as follows: In May-June I shall be in the U.S.A. to do the editing of my new book (to come out end of the year Jan. 1985 probably, because of the presidential elections which clutter up November and December and are a bad time for any book to come out). In September–October I shall be again in China, and am trying to work out a rather dilemma situation, in which I should be both in Peking and in Vancouver for a Convention at the same time....I haven't found yet the secret formula which enables one to be in two places at once; though you, Natwar, often seem able to take 20 hours of airplane travel and look none the worse for it, I can assure you it plays havoc with me.

I am starting another book this month of April, and intend

(Contd...)

to be working at it throughout 1984, and early 1985 I shall again be in the U.S. to promote the last book THE ENCHANTRESS, due out in January 1985, and to fix the contracts for the next one. What are your travel plans? Or perhaps there are so many that it is impossible to have a program for you? Anyway, I do hope to see you and if I pass thru India more than one day, will phone you. I was only one day in Delhi, and could not reach you on the phone, it was a Saturday... now I realize you were just then receiving the Padma Bhushan!!!

With much love to both of you, please keep in touch,

Suyin

(Han Suyin)

37 Montoie,
Lausanne,
Switzerland.

13 November 1984

Dearest Natwar and Hem,

We were both so grieved by the terrible thing that happened; we went to the ceremony here, which Ambassador Abraham conducted very well, but the loss is great. I hope that the Prime Minister Rajiv Gandhi will be able to master all the difficulties which seem to crop up; somehow or other, I feel that he needs not only the advice of his own group, but also of people like you, who are seasoned in diplomacy and in understanding of the world.

I have not written to him yet, thinking that this kind of letter-writing: at a time when he must be submerged with such things, will not be appropriate. When I do, I shall send it through you.

I am going to France for two weeks; my book is out in French translation BEFORE the English original, but this is customary. What are your plans? I am sure you must go on and that you will win in the elections. This is very important.

With so much love to you and to Hem, our hearts are with you as always,

Suyin

(Han Suyin)

3 January 1991

Dearest Natwar and Hem,

I was very happy to get your new phone numbers and address, as I had not heard from you for a long time. As you know, Vincent had a stroke in May, which left him paralyzed on the right side. He recovered well, had an operation, and is now totally fit, in fact much better than before. He also lost around 15 pounds, which was good for him.

All this was a bit of a strain, but everything went well.

I am completing my ZHOU ENLAI book, but decided to publish later, as a publication now would not get any attention, with the Gulf thing going on.

I am also writing another book on the story of the democracy movement in China...such as it is...

Some people complain that they have not enough work to do. I seem not to have enough time for all the work which I have to do.

We were in China October–November, Vincent and I, and visited the economic zones.

I was just asked today by a Swiss banker whether I thought that there would be war between Pakistan and India. I said that I did not think so. Now I am wondering WHY the question came up.

I shall not comment on the troubles in India. Both China and India still have loads of past history to digest and to work out of their systems.

I do hope all goes well with you and that you are finding the new government a fairly good one.

With much affection, as always, and all good wishes for the New Year.

Suyin

(Han Suyin)

37 Montoie,
Lausanne 1007,
Switzerland.

19 September 1991

My very dearest Natwar,

I am very sorry that I won't be available in November, things are rushing and crowding on me and November was just the month when I have to make sure that the ZHOU EN LAI biography, which is now ready, won't be botched up by the Americans.

I can't go into details, but we shall talk about it when we meet. With the new business and money above all mentality, all of us are being treated like salesmen. We have to "produce". A book is now called a "product". It makes me want to say bad words, like shit.

I can prepare a small speech, not too long, and send it to you to be read at the meeting which I cannot attend. Please let me know if this will be acceptable, as soon as possible.

With all warm affection, love, and friendship. I know what you are going through. You too, I am sure, know what I am going through for my country, China.

Suyin

(Han Suyin)

PS: Your letter of September 11 1991 arrived this morning ref iac 91 910450 (or 910480)

14 May 1993

Dearest Natwar,

It was quite a shock to me to read about the expulsion from Congress, or whatever, just because you did not agree with certain things.[1]

I read it in THE HINDU WEEKLY which only arrived today.

I do hope all is well with you.

Thank you for reviewing my book WIND IN MY SLEEVES. It does not matter that some people in the west pan it, I can take it, and it does not matter in the long run. I am not a short-distance runner.

Please do drop me a line.

Vincent has just had open heart surgery in Madras as he was not well when we went to China in April. The Indian surgeons were splendid. He had a heart attack on April 23, they operated him on May 6. I cannot tell you the anxiety, which now is allayed, for I am sure he will do very well. He will be out of hospital in a few days and back home and I shall go to India to pick him up as soon as he can travel.

With all love to you and to Hem,

Suyin

(Han Suyin)

---

[1]Four other Congressmen and I were suspended by P.V. Narasimha Rao for opposing him.

37 Montoie,
Lausanne 1007,
Switzerland.

5 March 1996

Dearest Natwar and Hem,

I am writing to you because I did not get any reply from you to my letter. Obviously, and I respect your judgement, you did not agree with my book on ZHOU ENLAI. It is now a best seller in Taiwan. But of course, this is another universe, the Chinese universe, just as there is the India universe. And I hope that India will do well and enter the 21st century as a major power.

Vincent and I were concerned about certain news[1] recently in the Indian newspapers about you. I cannot comment, except to say that for us, you are a dear friend and we do hope that everything will be cleared up.

This is 1996. It is exactly 40 years since we met in Beijing, and became good friends. I treasure the memory. It is also exactly 40 years that I met Vincent in Nepal.

I hope all will go well, and Vincent and I send you our faithful affection. And of course, also to Hem.

(Han Suyin)

---

[1] News about my loss in the Lok Sabha election from Bharatpur in 1996.